KAFKA'S PRAGUE

To Vera Saudková and Marianna Steiner

Kafka's Prague

Klaus Wagenbach

Translated by Ewald Osers with Peter Lewis

Introduction by Ritchie Robertson

First published in German in the Rowohlt monographien series as *Franz Kafka*
Copyright © 1964, 2002 Rowohlt Taschenbuch Verlag GmbH

First published in English in 2003 by Haus Publishing Ltd

This first paperback edition published in 2019 by
Armchair Traveller
4 Cinnamon Row
London SW11 3TW

Translation copyright © Ewald Osers, 2003
Introduction copyright © Ritchie Robertson, 2003

ISBN 978-1-909961-65-4

Typeset in Garamond by MacGuru Ltd
Printed in the United Kingdom by TJ International Ltd

www.hauspublishing.com
@hauspublishing.com

Contents

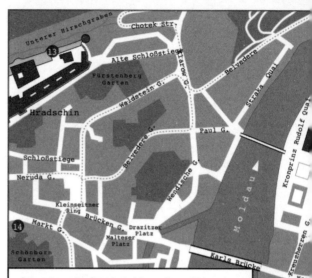

Orientation points for today's visitor to Prague. This map refers to the German names Kafka would have known. In brackets on this legend are today's Czech streets.

1. Only the entrance remains of the house at Rathausgasse 5 (U radnice), where Kafka was born
2. The shop of the Kafkas between 1896 and 1907 was located on Zeltnergasse 12 (Celetná)
3. House Minuta, Kleiner Ring 2 (Malé námestí)
4. Kafka's elementary school is now an apartment block on Fleischmarktgasse (Masná II/13)
5. The Kinsky Palace, which housed both the Gymnasium and, later, Kafka's father's shop, is on the Großer Altstädter Ring (Staromestské námestí)
6. The Kafka family home between 1869 and 1907 at Zeltnergasse 3
7. German students entered the Karolinum from the Eisengasse (Zelezná), the Czech used the entrance on the Obstmarkt (Ovocny trh)
8. The building housing the Assicurazioni Generali was located on the corner of the Wenzelsplatz (Václavské námestí) and the Heinrichgasse (Jindrisská)
9. The building of the Arbeiter-Unfall-Versicherungsanstalt (Poric 7) still exists
10. The house on Niklasstraße 36 (Parízská) had to make room for a hotel built on that spot
11. The room Kafka lived in Bilekgasse 10 (Bilkova) still exists
12. So does Lange Gasse 705/II (today Dlouhá 16)
13. The little house in the Alchimistengässchen can be found at Zlatá ulica 22
14. The Schönborn Palace in the Marktgasse 15 (Trziste) is now the American Embassy
15. The Oppelt-House is located on the corner of the Altstädter Ring (Staromestské námestí) and Niklasstraße (Parízská). The top floor was damaged during the Second World War. The entrance in Kafka's times was on Altstädter Ring 6 (now 5).

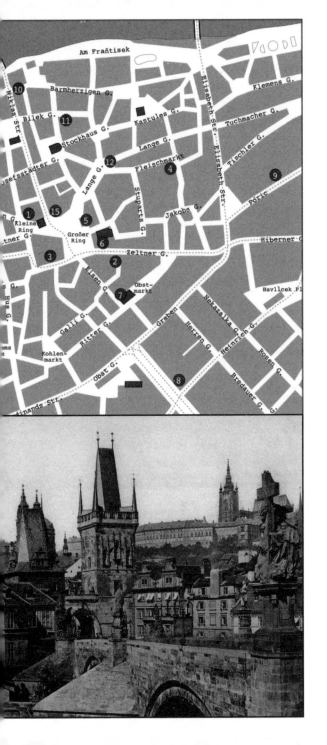

Dedicated to the memory of W G Sebald

Introduction

WHEN GERMAN LITERATURE has been presented to readers in English, the intermediaries have often been Scottish. Thomas Carlyle, who translated fiction by Goethe and the German Romantics, urged the early Victorian generation to discard the self-pity of Byron for the practical wisdom of Goethe. John Davidson, born in Greenock, was among the first British writers to absorb Nietzsche. And it was Willa and Edwin Muir, a couple who originated from the Shetland and Orkney islands respectively, who first translated Franz Kafka into English.

Not long after their marriage, the Muirs decided they could live more cheaply and more interestingly in central Europe than in post-war London. From August 1921 to March 1922 they lived in Prague (though they had not yet heard of Kafka), then moved to the artists' suburb of Hellerau outside Dresden – where they began learning German – and later to Salzburg and Vienna.

After returning to London in 1924, they managed to persuade Martin Secker to publish the unknown Franz Kafka. Their translation of *The Castle* appeared in 1930, followed by *The Trial* (1937), *America* (1938), and two volumes of shorter pieces. The credit for introducing Kafka to the English-speaking world goes primarily to Willa, who was much the more accurate linguist of the two. Their versions recreate Kafka's original in beautiful, simple, natural English, but contain some absurd mistakes, mostly resulting from their unfamiliarity with German idioms. Thus, in *The Trial*, K is made to tell the court: 'You scoundrels, I'll give you all an inter-rogation yet', instead of 'You scoundrels! You can keep all your hearings!'[1]

It was a long time before Kafka found a large British readership: in the 1930s, none of his books sold more than a few hundred copies. After 1940, however, sales increased markedly, and by the end of the decade Kafka was recognised as a key modern author. In 1953, Penguin Books published a paperback edition of *The Trial* and by 1966 it had sold 200,000 copies.[2]

Inevitably, initial responses to Kafka were guided by the religious interpretation put forward by Max Brod, who, as Kafka's closest friend and the editor of his novels, spoke with some authority. However, Brod increasingly made Kafka's writings serve his own aim of revitalising modern Judaism in association with Zionism, and insisted on deriving from them a positive message that other readers failed to find. Edwin Muir's introduction to *The Castle* is consider-ably more agnostic: 'In the present book and in *The Trial*, the pos-tulates [Kafka] begins with are the barest possible; they are roughly these: that there is a right way of life, and that the discovery of it depends on one's attitude to powers which are almost unknown.'[3]

As one looks through the British reactions to Kafka assembled by Dieter Jakob, one sees increasing discomfort with the religious interpretation of Kafka's fiction. His inscrutable authorities seem too arbitrary, cruel or ludicrous to represent divinity, unless divin-ity is imagined as evil. By the 1940s, Kafka was widely seen not as a religious prophet but as a forerunner of existentialism, giving fictional form to the metaphysical uncertainty and spiritual home-lessness that was considered characteristic of modern man. Such an approach is more plausible than the certainties ascribed to him by Brod. In 1917, Kafka himself wrote: 'I was not led into life by the sinking hand of Christianity, like Kierkegaard, nor did I catch the last tip of the Jewish prayer-shawl before it flew away, like the Zionists. I am the end or the beginning.'[4]

Some readers also wanted a political understanding of Kafka. To them, his depictions of authority, though appallingly convincing, lacked any possibility of resistance. In 1935, Stephen Spender wrote of Kafka: 'His vision of society is authoritative, ironically religious, and nihilist.'[5] Not only in the 1930s and 1940s, but also, and even more, during the Cold War, Kafka seemed to have envisaged totalitarianism with uncanny accuracy. Thus, in 1954 a reviewer asked: 'Joseph K., the bank clerk in *The Trial* who is charged with a crime of which he is totally unaware, arrested by the decree of authorities whom he did not know existed, who remains ignorant of his offence even when he is executed, is he not the universal victim of the purge trial, the concentration camp, and the gas-chamber, one denied not only human, but also divine, justice?'[6]

The cliché of Kafka as prophet of totalitarianism is persistent. But rather than ascribing to Kafka, who died in 1924, supernatural abilities, it would be more pertinent to reflect that totalitarian states operate through a perverted bureaucracy, and that Kafka, as an employee of a quasi-governmental body, the Workers' Accident Insurance Institute, had ample experience of bureaucracy and its absurdities. Reviewing *The Trial* in 1937, Edward Sackville-West declared: 'Anyone who has attempted to deal with a central European post or customs office will recognise at once the milieu from which Kafka drew his astonishing vision of human existence: the dusty room ... the cross officials, delighting in causing as much trouble as possible, the sense of absolute timelessness, the irritable boredom and tyranny.'[7] This aspect of Kafka's life, which proved so fertile for his imagination, is documented by Klaus Wagenbach, who was the first person to republish the official reports on safety standards in factories that Kafka wrote for the Insurance Institute's yearbook. To Kafka's chagrin, these often remained unread, like the mounds of documents that accumulate in the offices of the comically inefficient bureaucrats in *The Castle*.

Kafka's vision of threatening and pointless bureaucracy has since been encapsulated in the English word 'Kafkaesque'. The earliest citation given in the *Oxford English Dictionary* is from the *New Yorker* of January 1947: 'A Kafkaesque nightmare of blind alleys'; but the word seems to have been used first in 1938 by Cecil Day Lewis, who described Edward Upward's novel *Journey to the Border* as 'Kafkaesque in manner'.[8] By 1947, the word must already have been widespread, for later that year Edmund Wilson wrote: 'Kafka's novels have exploited a vein of the comedy and pathos of futile effort which is likely to make "Kafkaesque" a permanent word.'[9]

Kafka's distinctive tone pervades modern literature. It is present in Camus, Sartre, Robbe-Grillet, Beckett, Borges and many others.[10] One can distinguish broadly between those who react to Kafka solemnly and those who respond to the comedy and pathos that Wilson noted. Among the latter, my own favourite is Jorge Luis Borges, whose story 'The Lottery in Babylon' not only develops Kafka's image of inscrutable authorities but also pays him an unusual tribute by mentioning how information about the all-powerful Lottery Company is said to be deposited in 'a sacred latrine called Qaphqa'.[11] Borges has also pointed out how Kafka affects even the literature of the past. Once one has read Kafka, much in earlier writing looks Kafkaesque *avant la lettre*. Borges finds examples in the pre-Socratic philosophers, in Chinese myths, in the biography of Kierkegaard, and in Robert Browning.

A similar insight underlies one of the earliest essays on Kafka, by the great German-Jewish critic Walter Benjamin, who begins with a Kafkaesque anecdote from the Russian bureaucracy under Catherine the Great. Potemkin, her notoriously drunken minister, was at last induced by the devoted clerk Shuvalkin to sign a sheaf of belated documents. But after bearing them back to his office in triumph, the

4

clerk discovered that on each one Potemkin had written the name 'Shuvalkin'. [12]

Among British writers in the 1930s, even those who disapproved of Kafka's political quietism admired his narrative method, variously called allegorical or symbolic. Julian Symons thought this method could inspire 'anti-Fascist fairy tales of great power and beauty'. [13] The best-known attempts, *The Wild Goose Chase* (1937) and *The Aerodrome* (1941) by Rex Warner, are infused with images of an impenetrable organisation headed by mysterious figures of authority such as the Air Vice-Marshal. It may be tempting to imagine Kafka's presence behind Orwell's *Nineteen Eighty-four*, but this grim, obsessive dystopia lacks both Kafka's ambiguity and his humour; its main literary model is Yevgeny Zamyatin's *We*.

Writers inspired by Kafka's supposed depiction of totalitarianism tend to signal their allegiance by giving their protagonists initials, as J G Ballard does with 'M' in the story 'The Concentration City' (from *The Disaster Area*, 1967), and J M Coetzee does when describing the racial persecution of white-ruled South Africa in *The Life and Times of Michael K* (1983).

Alasdair Gray's *Lanark* comes helpfully equipped with an 'Index of Plagiarisms', which includes the image of a human shape outlined against a lit window, taken from the last chapter of *The Trial*. [14] But the 'plagiarisms' Gray acknowledges may well veil other sources of inspiration. The sinister medical institute in the first part of *Lanark* looks like another Kafka-inspired organisation; while in the fourth part, the surreally accelerated relationship between Lanark and Rima, whose baby is born and grows up within a few hours, resembles that between K and Frieda in *The Castle* both in its outward absurdity and in its poignant atmosphere of emotional failure.

Increasing knowledge of his life added another element to Kafka's legacy. His diaries were published in English translation in 1948 and 1949. The letters to Milena Jesenská soon followed, as did Gustav

Janouch's *Conversations with Kafka* (the latter a rather unreliable source). Max Brod's biography, first published in 1937, appeared in English in 1947. All this material focused attention on Kafka the person. Kafka's notoriously difficult relationship with his father attracted the interest of Nadine Gordimer, who imagined how it might have looked from Hermann Kafka's point of view.[15] Maggie Ross made Kafka's lover Milena Jesenská the central figure of a novel (*Milena*, 1983) in which it only gradually becomes apparent that the heroine's unsatisfactory and perplexing lover 'Frank' is to be identified with Kafka. And J P Stern, unsympathetic to the 1930s view of Kafka as insufficiently political, imagined what might have happened if Kafka, instead of dying of tuberculosis, had survived, received an early-morning call from the Gestapo, escaped and joined the Czech partisans.[16]

These biographical materials also highlight the sheer ordinariness of Kafka's life. Unlike the many modern writers who have lived nomadic or bohemian lives, Kafka turned out to have held down a real job for some 14 years as a valued employee of the Workers' Accident Insurance Institute. Comparisons with T S Eliot, who worked in a bank before becoming a publisher, with the insurance lawyer Wallace Stevens, and even with the university librarian Philip Larkin, come readily to mind.

Kafka's difficulties with parents and partners, though described in extreme language, were not so very remote from many people's experience. His personal documents, too, turned out to be full of pleasingly mundane detail. Thus, on meeting the artist Alfred Kubin, Kafka devoted most space to recording Kubin's advice about laxatives. Kafka's life revealed a 'Larkinesque' aspect, encouraging what Alan Bennett calls 'the temptation to "English" Kafka and joke him down to size'.[17] Roy Fuller, in his novel *Image of a Society* (1956), wanted to depict a writer who worked as a lawyer in a large organisation, and drew on the case of Kafka: 'I had to transfer the chap from pre-First World War Prague to post-Second World War "Saddleford", but the process brought out the sordid and ludicrous elements in such a life (and I did not attempt to underplay them) which the passage of time and the abstracting process of literary biography (and, indeed, Kafka's fiction itself) have tended to remove from Kafka's real life.' [18]

The Larkinesque side of Kafka has been most visible in other media. Films and plays based on Kafka's texts are numerous.[19] Though the best known may be Orson Welles's *The Trial* (1963), I much prefer the less portentous 1993 version directed by Terry Jones based on a screenplay by Harold Pinter, which renders the fictional world of Kafka's novel in captivatingly sordid detail, with the artist Titorelli as a suitably dodgy salesman. Pinter said that the two writers who had made most impact on him were Kafka and Beckett, and in *The Homecoming* he treated the relationship between father and son in a manner that unavoidably recalls Kafka.[20]

Kafka's Dick, a play by Alan Bennett himself, transports Kafka and Brod into the living room of a suburban couple, where the husband works in the insurance business and is writing an article about Kafka for '*Small Print*, the Journal of Insurance Studies'.[21] Possibly the best part of the play is the 'Prologue', in which the dying Kafka tells Brod to burn his writings and is then horrified by the prospect that, if Brod obeys, his works will not be available to be burnt by the Nazis – a brilliant exposure of literary vanity.

Bennett focuses on Kafka's professional life again in the television drama *The Insurance Man* (set in Prague and shot in Bradford) in which a young man with a mysterious skin disease, apparently from his job in a dyeworks, comes to the Workers' Accident Insurance Institute to claim compensation, and is offered by the rather superior official Kafka a job in the asbestos factory which actually did belong to Kafka's brother-in-law. Bennett has drawn on what the translated sources can tell him about Kafka's office work, and on Kafka's fiction, so that Kafka is blended with his own fictional 'Country Doctor', and the young man with the skin disease recalls the young man in that story with the inexplicable wound whom the Doctor is unable to cure. While *Kafka's Dick* plays hilariously with images of Kafka, *The Insurance Man* enters not only into Kafka's life but into his imagination, and is both creation and criticism. With a truly Kafkaesque blend of humour and seriousness, it examines the life of a bureaucrat who has become famous not least as a satirist of bureaucracy.

Kafka's literary afterlife is inseparable from his life story. Although critical dogma often tries to sever text from life, the experience of readers is that acquaintance with an author's life enhances the understanding of fiction, as the constant demand for literary biographies shows. Knowledge of Kafka's life reveals the reality in which his fiction is anchored, and his personal writings, liberally quoted by Wagenbach, disclose, along with intermittent desperation, and even during it, a quiet humour that can also be found throughout his fiction. And though Kafka, in his last story, 'Josephine the Singer or the Mouse People', celebrated the oblivion into which the artist would fall, his life and his fiction together ensure that he continues to fascinate.

RITCHIE ROBERTSON
St John's College, Oxford

1

Fame – Too Late for the Author

FRANZ KAFKA GAVE US some of the most haunting literary images of the 20th century. The commercial traveller Gregor Samsa in *The Metamorphosis*, who wakes up one morning to find himself transformed in his bed into a gigantic insect.[1] The son who carries out the sentence imposed by his father, and throws himself off a bridge in *The Judgement*. Young Karl, who blunders through America, much as the elderly country doctor blunders through the 'unhappiest of ages'.[2] Josef K in *The Trial*, who is arrested despite having committed no crime. The officer from *In the Penal Colony* who lovingly describes his torture machine. Red Peter, who reports to the esteemed gentlemen of the academy on his past life as an ape. The dead hunter, Gracchus, and his vain search for peace. The futile art of Josephine the singing mouse.

The creator of these images was not a well-travelled man. His life lacked the constant changes of scene that characterise so many writers' biographies of the 20th century. It lacked the long journeys, the formative experiences and their consequences. It lacked important encounters with fellow writers. Kafka did not even know many of his most important Austrian contemporaries. He knew their work, of course – he was an enthusiastic if unsystematic reader – but he excluded himself from literary discussions. At best he was a

Prague. View of the Charles Bridge and the Hradshin Castle.

monosyllabic and reticent listener to such conversations. He usually sent his manuscripts to periodicals and publishers only when invited to do so, and he limited his contacts to a select few friends. It was an essentially provincial existence – a 'local' one, like that of the Austrian novelist Adalbert Stifter (1805–68) or the Irish poet W B Yeats (1865–1939).

Franz Kafka was born in Prague on 3 July 1883, rarely left his native city (and then only for brief periods) and, after a short life of almost 41 years, was buried there at the *Straschnitzer Friedhof* (Strašnice, now usually called Olšany cemetery). For 14 years he worked as a lawyer for the Workers' Accident Insurance Institute for the Kingdom of Bohemia, although he regarded his 'scribbling' in the evening or at night as his 'sole desire'.[3]

The prose written by this Prague Jew outside office hours gained international recognition only after the Second World War. Kafka's fame began with a small circle of German literary experts in the 1920s. He was especially promoted in France, first by André Breton (1896–1966) and the group involved with *Minotaure* magazine, later Albert Camus (1913–60) and Jean-Paul Sartre (1905–80); and eventually Kafka became established in Britain and America. It was not until the 1950s that his work 'came back' to German literature, when the first 'official' German *Collected Works* appeared in the early years of that decade. And it was not until 1957 that the first Czech translations were published in Prague, the city that Kafka had put on the literary map. The first Russian translation of his work ('In the Penal Colony') appeared in 1964. Only 40 years after the author's death in 1924 could it be said that his work was being read all over the world.

The facts about Kafka's life were not known until much later, even though he lived during the entirely transparent final three decades of the Habsburg monarchy and the first years of the Czechoslovak Republic. This was due not only to the fact that his life was inconspicuous, but also because of the political events of the years from 1933 to 1945. These years, above all, concerned his writing: at the beginning of the 1930s, during a search of the Berlin flat of Dora Diamant (the companion of Kafka's last years), the Gestapo confiscated a number of manuscripts, which must now be considered lost. The first collected edition of his work, begun in Germany in 1935, was obstructed and then prohibited. Far worse events followed the occupation of Czechoslovakia by the Nazis: Kafka's three sisters were deported to a concentration camp and murdered – a fate shared by many of his relatives and friends. Archives were destroyed; documents were lost; witnesses of his life were killed.

In 1957, when I first visited Prague, I was faced with a sad yet consoling picture: the image of an undamaged city, one of the most beautiful in Europe, but also a very confused picture. On the one hand, almost all of the buildings in which Kafka lived or worked have survived – the Kinsky and the Schönborn Palaces, the Minutá House, and the Oppelt House, the houses at Bilková 10, *Zeltnergasse* (Celetná) 3 and *Lange Gasse* (Dlouhá) 18, the office building at *Pořič* (Na Porící) 7, and the little house in the *Alchimistengasse* (Zlatá ulička). The same is true in provincial Bohemia, in *Wossek* (Osek), *Podiebrad* (Poděbrady), *Triesch* (now Třešt), *Schelesen* (now Želízy) and in Matliary in Slovakia. On the other hand, time and again my search for documents ended in plundered archives; my search for surviving witnesses almost always ended in a room of the Jewish Town Hall on the *Maiselgasse* (Maislová ulice), the walls of which held shelves filled with hundreds of card indices containing individual red cards listing first name, surname and place of birth – all invariably bore the same rubber stamp: Oświęcim – AUSCHWITZ.

2

The Son of a Shopkeeper, Lost in Prague

K AFKA HAS NOT CONTRIBUTED MUCH to the illumination of his everyday life, even though his diaries and letters – in total almost 3,000 pages – are more extensive than his literary work. His only major autobiographical statement is the 'Letter to his Father' from his later years (1919), a vain attempt 'to reassure us both [Kafka and his father] a little and make our living and our dying easier'.[1] However, Kafka's desire in this letter to 'reassure' his father – who viewed his son's writing with suspicion and incomprehension – led him to falsify many of the facts, and Kafka himself, a year later, referred to the 'lawyer's tricks' of this letter.[2]

His other autobiographical remarks are less dishonest, but there are few of them and they are mostly no more than marginal comments of self-criticism. Only once does Kafka speak of his ancestors:

In Hebrew my name is Amschel, like my mother's maternal grandfather [Amschel or Adam Porias], whom my mother, who was six years old when he died, can remember as a very pious and learned man with a long white beard. She remembers how she had to take hold of the toes of the corpse and ask forgiveness for any offence she might have committed against her grandfather. She also remembers her grandfather's many

Kafka's father, Hermann (c.1883).

books which lined the walls. He bathed in the river every day, even in winter, when he chopped a hole in the ice for his bath. My mother's mother [Esther Porias] died of typhus at an early age. From the time of this death her grandmother [Sara Porias] became melancholic, refused to eat, spoke with no one. Once, a year after the death of her daughter, she went for a walk and did not return – her body was found in the Elbe. An even more learned man than her grandfather was my mother's great-grandfather, Christians and Jews held him in equal honour; during a fire a miracle took place as a result of his piety, the flames jumped over and spared his house while the houses around it burned down. He had four sons, one converted to Christianity and became a doctor. All but my mother's grandfather died young. He had one son, whom my mother knew as crazy Uncle Nathan, and one daughter, my mother's mother.[3]

Strangely enough, there exists a kind of companion piece to this diary entry by Kafka – two hand-written sheets by his mother, on which, some 15 years after her son's note, this woman of 77 (in 1932) provides a brief biography:

My dear deceased husband came from *Wossek* near *Strakonitz* [Strakonice]. His father was a big, powerful man. He was a butcher, but did not live to a great age. His wife, my mother-in-law [Franziska], had six children, four sons and two daughters. She was a delicate, hardworking woman, who, despite all trouble and difficulties, brought up her children well and they were the only happiness in her life. My husband was sent away as a boy of 14 and had to fend for himself. In his 20th year, he became a soldier, rising to platoon leader. In his 30th year, he married me. He had set himself up with modest financial means and, since we were both very hard working, made a respected name for himself. We had six children, of whom only three daughters are still alive.

Our eldest son Franz was a delicate but healthy child. He was born in 1883 and died on 3 June 1924. Two years later we had another little son, who was called Georg. He was a pretty, vigorous child and died of measles in his second year. Then came the third child, again a boy. He died of an inflammation of his middle ear at barely six months. He was called Heinrich. Our three daughters are happily married and all three live in Prague.

I was born in *Bad Poděbrad* [Poděbrady]. My grandfather, my mother's father, was an educated man with a Jewish education. Name of Porias. He was a devout Jew and a well-known Talmud scholar. He had a successful drapery shop in *Poděbrad*, which was greatly neglected because grandfather preferred to busy himself with the Talmud. The grandparents had a fine single-storey house on the Ringplatz [now Staroměstské náměstí]. The shop was on the ground floor and the best room on the first floor was filled with all kinds of scholarly books. Grandfather was a highly respected man and died at a ripe old age. He had, as I heard in my childhood, two brothers. One of them was very religious. He wore the tassels of his prayer shawl over his coat, even though the school children ran after him and laughed at him. They were reprimanded at school and the children were strictly instructed by their teacher not to bother the holy man, or else they would be very severely punished. In summer as well as in winter he went bathing in the Elbe every day. In winter, when there was a frost, he had a pickaxe with which he hacked open the ice in order to submerge himself. The third brother of my grandfather was a doctor and had had himself baptised. My mother was the only child of the eldest, the religious Talmud scholar. She died of typhus aged 28, leaving, in addition to myself who was only three years old, three brothers. My father married again after a year, and by the second marriage there were my two brothers. One died in the war [in] his 60th year, the other is a doctor. As my brothers were all away, my parents sold the house, and also the shop, and moved to Prague.

My second mother [Julie] died 12 years ago at the age of 81; my father two years later at the age of 86. Father was born in *Humpoletz* [Humpolec], worked as a cloth-maker and married my mother, who received the house in *Poděbrad* and also the shop as a dowry.

Father had four brothers and one sister. The brothers were rich people, they owned several textile factories, instead of Löwy they were called Lauer and had been baptised. My father's youngest nephew was the owner of a brewery in *Koschieř* [Košíře]. He was baptised and was also called Lauer instead of Löwy. He died in his 56th year. I had five brothers. The eldest

Kafka's mother, Julie, *née* Löwy (c.1883).

lived many years in Madrid as the bank manager of two railways. He was a highly respected official, had many decorations and was esteemed by all who knew him. Because of his position he had been obliged to be baptised. He was single and died in 1923 and was buried in Madrid. My second brother is a businessman, the third was abroad for many years, to wit 12 years in the Central Congo, in China and in Japan.[4]

It is significant that Kafka, in his diary entry, mentions only the ancestors on his mother's side: their inherited traits were clearly dominant in him. Also, it was the maternal ancestors of his mother that lived in the small Bohemian town of *Poděbrad*. Among them, time and again, we find pious scholars and rabbis living a retiring existence, a few doctors, and numerous bachelors and eccentrics, often regarded by their community as odd, often with the delicate constitution that Kafka inherited. His mother's paternal ancestors, on the other hand, belonged to the textile families common in Bohemia and Moravia, 'enlightened' people of moderate Jewish Orthodoxy.

Kafka's maternal grandparents clearly reflect the religious divergence of the times: grandfather Jakob Löwy was 'assimilated', while grandmother Esther came from a strictly observant family. After bearing her fourth child, Esther (as Kafka's mother reports) died of typhus, in 1859. Yet the suicide of Esther's mother reported by Kafka was probably caused by other factors as well: Jakob Löwy remarried a mere year after his first wife's death, and this may have led Esther's mother (Kafka's great-grandmother) to take her own life. Therefore, the mother and both grandparents of Kafka's mother Julie (born in 1856) died early, and from her fourth year she grew up under the care of her stepmother and her father. This second marriage produced two sons, and the lives of the six siblings once more reflect the peculiarity of this family.

Julie's eldest brother, Alfred (Kafka's 'Madrid uncle') remained a bachelor and eventually rose to become the manager of a Spanish railway company. Another brother, Josef, likewise emigrated: he worked for a large Belgian colonial company in the Congo and in China, married and later lived in Paris (after which Kafka referred to him as his 'Parisian uncle'). The third brother, Richard, became a merchant, led an entirely unremarkable life and had three children. The stepbrother, Siegfried (Kafka's favourite uncle), was a peculiar eccentric, a fresh-air fanatic, educated, well-read (he was the only one in the entire family to possess a large library), witty, ready to help and benign, though outwardly he appeared to be 'a little cold'.[5] He remained a bachelor and became a country doctor in *Triesch* (Třešt), Moravia, where Kafka later often visited him. The second stepbrother, Rudolf, likewise a bachelor, lived a retiring life as an accountant in the *Košíře* brewery. He was the oddest and most private of Kafka's uncles. He converted to Catholicism and, as Kafka recorded, progressively developed into an 'indecipherable, excessively modest, solitary, and yet almost loquacious man'.[6] Some of these qualities were also very marked in Kafka himself, especially the shy, almost over-anxious modesty, his timidity, and a certain poverty of human contact. 'Touchiness, a sense of justice, restlessness',[7] is how Kafka characterised the inherited Löwy traits.

By comparison, Kafka's paternal heritage was slight. His father, Hermann, was born in 1852 in *Wossek*, southern Bohemia, a tiny village of scarcely a hundred inhabitants. Hermann came from a humble background: his father, Jakob, was a butcher. In 1849, rather late in life, at the age of 35, Jakob Kafka married his neighbour Franziska Platowski. Apparently, this delay had something to do with a change in the marriage laws. Until 1848, when Jews were granted certain basic rights, only the eldest child in a Jewish family could marry. After 1848, there was a general drift of Jews from provincial Bohemia to the more 'liberal' towns. For this reason, when Jakob died 40 years later, he was the last Jew in his native village. He had six children, two daughters and four sons; they became merchants, or married merchants, in *Strakonitz* (Strakonice), *Kolin* (Kolín), *Leitmeritz* (Litoměřice), *Schüttenhofen* (Sušice) and Prague respectively.

The Kafka family lived in extremely modest circumstances. All of them, while still very young, had to take meat to the neighbouring villages in a handcart, early in the morning, even in winter, and often barefoot. Their house was a type of cottage common in Bohemia, barely higher than a man, and consisted of two ground-floor rooms with low ceilings, in which the family of eight lived. Schooling, given the circumstances, seems to have been above average. *Wossek* then still had a Jewish school – a remnant from when the village had a large Jewish community – where Kafka's father, who in those days spoke primarily Czech, presumably learned to read and write German. Even so, it was only a basic education: the letters of the

30-year-old Hermann to his fiancée contain numerous mistakes and their style is clearly modelled on a letter-writing guide.

At the age of 14, Hermann Kafka left *Wossek* to seek his fortune as an itinerant trader and travelling salesman, evidently with some success. After his military service, he moved to Prague and within a few years set up a fashion accessories shop, no doubt with financial help from his more affluent bride, Julie Löwy, the daughter of a brewer.* The Kafka 'will to life, business and conquest'⁸ was very

---

*There has been a Jewish community living in Prague from at least 1091 AD. When Kafka was born, Prague and its suburbs were home to nearly 500,000 people. The city was part of the Austro-Hungarian Empire, which covered a vast part of central and eastern Europe. Emperor Franz Josef included Serbs, Slovaks, Poles, Czechs and Croats among his subjects. But Prague was only the third city in the Dual Monarchy of Austria and Hungary; the capital cities of Vienna and Budapest were the real seats of power within this multinational empire.

The population of Prague was almost 90 per cent Catholic. The rest were Jewish, some 26,000 in 1900, most of whom were middle class and spoke German, the official mother tongue of the empire. Indeed, under Franz Josef there had been a concerted attempt to Germanise the lands under Habsburg control, leading to considerable resentment amongst the disparate ethnic groups that made up the empire. In Prague, 80 per cent of the population was Czech-speaking, yet the German-speaking minority dominated the media and the institutions of higher education. Ethnically, Prague was a divided city.

Among the city's Jewish community there was a strong tradition of assimilation. Kafka's father spoke both Czech and German. But Jewish traditions were neglected in the Kafka household, and Franz would later resent his lack of Jewish roots. The Kafkas remained on the fringes of both Czech and Jewish communities in Prague. Growing Czech nationalism and the anti-Semitism inherent in the Austro-Hungarian Empire both had the effect of marginalising the Jews.

By 1900, the Dual Monarchy was under strain from nationalist conflicts. The traditional Habsburg joke had been 'the situation is desperate, but not serious'. Now this sounded increasingly hollow. In Prague, as elsewhere in the empire, nationalism caught the imagination of the people, and in 1918, after its

strong in Hermann, more so than in his brothers, who were 'all more cheerful, fresher, more informal, more easygoing, less severe'.[9]

Hermann Kafka never forgot his difficult youth, continually reminded his children of it, and considered social recognition the only worthwhile aim in life. In the old Austro-Hungarian provincial capital of Prague, it was only possible to achieve real social status by gaining access to the narrow German-speaking upper class. (In 1900, of the city's 450,000 inhabitants, only 34,000 spoke German.)

For a man like Kafka's father, this was no simple journey, even if one disregards the difficulties facing him as a Jew living with the still relatively mild anti-Semitism prevalent in Austria-Hungary. The principal obstacle was not his class or even his Jewishness, but the fact that he came from the Czech provinces, and that during his first years in Prague he still considered himself a Czech and was regarded as one. Thus, during that period, he was on the board of the first Prague synagogue to preach in Czech (the synagogue in *Heinrichgasse* (Jindřišská), founded c.1890). However, a short time later Hermann Kafka 'turned' into a political nobody, an opportunist. He switched to the congregation of the *Zigeuner* (Cikán) synagogue and later to that of the *Pinkas* synagogue. His occupational description in the Prague address book of 1907 – dealer in haberdashery, fashion articles, accessories, parasols, umbrellas, walking sticks, cotton – is followed by the smug 'Sworn expert at the law court'.

At this time his business logo showed a jackdaw (*kavka* in Czech) perching on an oak branch, a German national symbol, but he replaced it later with a less well-defined piece of foliage. The clearest indication of Hermann's determination to attach himself to German society was the education of his children, all of whom, without exception, went to German schools.

---

defeat in the First World War, the Habsburg monarchy ended, the empire broke up, and an independent Czechoslovak Republic was proclaimed.

Jackdaw (*kavka* in Czech).

The disparate backgrounds of Kafka's parents – a reflection of the social and linguistic mix of old Bohemia – emerges once more from the record of the marriage between Hermann Kafka and Julie Löwy in the Prague register of marriages for September 1882. Hermann, coming from the Czech-Jewish provincial proletariat, lived in Prague with his cousin on the edge of what had been a ghetto 20 years before. Julie, coming from the affluent and educated German-Jewish bourgeoisie, lived in one of the most beautiful houses on the *Altstädter Ring*, the 'Smetana House'. Franz Kafka was born a year later, on 3 July 1883, on the exact boundary of these two neighbourhoods, in the tenement building 'At the Tower', I/27, which belonged to the prelateship of St Nicholas – as if to assert the disparity of his origins once more.

Kafka's mixed origins also separate him from the other writers of the 'Prague school'. He was one of the few who spoke and wrote good Czech, and he was the only one who grew up in the centre of the Old Town, on the edge of the ghetto district, which still existed as a distinct area, with its own characteristic style of building. Kafka never forgot the atmosphere of his youth. Gustav Janouch, who befriended Kafka in 1920, reports him as saying:

> In us all it still lives – the dark corners, the secret alleys,
> shuttered windows, squalid courtyards, rowdy pubs and sinister
> inns. We walk through the broad streets of the newly-built

town. But our steps and glances are uncertain. Inside we tremble
just as before in the ancient streets of our misery. Our heart
knows nothing of the slum clearance that has been achieved.
The unhealthy old Jewish town within us is far more real than
the new hygienic town around us.[10]

Throughout his life – except during his final years, when his
illness compelled him to stay in sanatoria – Kafka rarely left this
innermost area of Prague's Old Town. 'One day, as we were looking
down from a window to the Town Square,' reports a witness, 'he
said, pointing to the buildings: "There was my *Gymnasium* [second-
ary school], over there, in the building that faces towards us, was
the university, and a short way to the left was my office. Within this
small circle" – drawing a few circles with his finger – "my whole life
is enclosed."' [11]

This enclosedness, this limitation of a person's living space, was
not all that unusual then. Admittedly, the Kafka family had to live
especially modestly during its early days in Prague. For the first
seven years after the foundation of the business, their flats were very
small and they moved frequently: *Wenzelplatz* (Václavské náměstí)
56, *Geistgasse* (Dušní) V/187, *Zeltnergasse* (Celetná) 3, *Niklasstraße*
(Mikulášská) 36 (now Pařížká třída 36) … All these addresses were
within, or close to, the Old Town, as was their first larger flat, into
which the family moved in June 1889, in the four-storey medieval
Minutá House (*Altstädter Ring* 2; between the two Old Town
Squares: the *Kleiner Ring* (Malé náměstí) and the bigger *Großer
Ring* (Staroměstské náměstí)), the back of which leans against the
Old Town Hall. Kafka's sisters were born in this house: Elli (1889),
Valli (1890) and Ottla (1892).

The *Kleiner Ring* and the streets and passages radiating from it,
with their narrow inner courtyards lined with open balconies called
'*Pawlatschen*' ('pavláče'), were the playground of the child Kafka.

It was also from the Minutá House that, in the autumn of 1889, he first walked to school, to the *Deutsche Knabenschule*, a German boys' school on the *Fleischmarkt* (Masnýtrh). Some 30 years later, in a letter to his friend and lover, Czech journalist Milena Jesenská, Kafka reveals the strength of these childhood impressions:

Our cook, a small, dry thin person with a pointed nose and hollow cheeks, yellowish but firm, energetic and superior, led me every morning to school. [...] We lived in the house that separates the Kleiner Ring from the Großer Ring. Thus, we walked first across the Ring, then into Teingasse [Týnská], then through a kind of archway in the Fleischmarktgasse [Masná] down to the Fleischmarkt. And now every morning for about a year the same thing was repeated. At the moment of leaving the house, the cook said she would tell the teacher how naughty I'd been at home. As a matter of fact, I probably wasn't very naughty, but rather stubborn, useless, sad, bad-tempered, and out of all this probably something quite nice could have been fabricated for the teacher. I knew this, so didn't take the cook's threats too lightly. All the same, because the road to school at first seemed enormously long to me, I believed that anything might happen on the way (it's from such apparent childish light-heartedness that there gradually develops, just because the roads are not so enormously long, this anxiousness and dead-eyed seriousness). I was also very much in doubt, at least while still on the Altstädter Ring [Staroměstské náměstí], as to whether the cook, though a person commanding respect if only in domestic quarters, would dare to talk to the world-respect-commanding person of the teacher. Perhaps I even mentioned something of this kind, whereupon the cook usually answered curtly with her thin merciless lips that I didn't have to believe it, but say it she would. Somewhere near the entrance to the Fleischmarktgasse (it still has a minor historical significance for me, in which neighbourhood did you live as a child?) the fear of the threat got the upper hand. School in itself was already enough of a nightmare, and now the cook was trying to make it even worse. I began to plead, she shook her head, the more I pleaded the more precious appeared to me that for which I was pleading, the greater the danger; I stood still and begged for forgiveness, she dragged me along, I threatened her with retaliation from my parents, she laughed, here she was all-powerful. I held on to the shop doors, to the corner stones, I refused to go any further until she had forgiven me. I pulled her back by the skirt (she didn't have it easy, either), but she kept dragging me along with the assurance that she would tell the teacher this, too; it grew late, the clock on the Jakobskirche [Kostel sv. Jakuba] struck eight, the school bells could be heard, other children began to run and all the time the thought: she'll tell, she won't tell – well, she didn't tell, ever, but she always had the opportunity and even an apparently increasing opportunity (I didn't tell yesterday, but I'll certainly tell today) and of this she never let go.[12]

The child's 'anxiousness' and 'dead-eyed seriousness', evident also from the early photographs, stem from the upbringing he received from his parents, insofar as there was such a thing. People then did not concern themselves greatly with the problems of raising children and the Kafkas certainly did not. The boy grew up in the care of cooks, nursemaids and servants. They were later joined by the domestic factotum Marie Werner, a Czech who lived with the Kafka family for decades and was universally known as *slečna* or 'Miss'. Added to these 'persons of standing' there was later also (as was *de rigeur* in Prague's 'better' families) a French governess.

Kafka rarely saw his parents: his father turned his shop into a

The ten-year-old Kafka with his sisters Elli (centre) and Valli.

noisy, and ever expanding, home from home; and his mother was obliged to be permanently in attendance on her husband, as an assistant and a moderating influence with regard to the employees, whom Kafka's father viewed as 'beasts, dogs' and 'paid enemies'. [13] Parental care was limited to instructions and orders at the table, since his mother had to keep his father company in the evenings as well, during the 'usual game of cards, accompanied by exclamations, laughter and squabbling, not to mention whistling'.[14]

In this 'oppressive, poison-laden, child-consuming air of the nicely furnished family room'[15] the boy grew up, his father's curt commands remaining to him incomprehensible or mysterious. He eventually became 'so unsure of everything that, in fact, I possessed only what I actually had in my hands or in my mouth or what was at least on the way there'.[16] A major contribution to this uncertainty was the way in which his father brought him up, which Kafka describes in 'Letter to his Father' as follows: 'You can only treat a child in the way you yourself are constituted, with vigour, noise and hot temper, and in this case this seemed to you, into the bargain, extremely suitable, because you wanted to bring me up to be a strong brave boy.'[17]

Faced by such demands, the opposing forces – his delicate and sensitive side bequeathed to him by his mother's ancestors – stood little chance, especially as the child (in the opinion, as Kafka bitterly records in his diary, of a 'former governess') was 'obedient, […] of a quiet disposition and good'.[18] The world outside was just as difficult to understand. Only on the surface did the Prague of that time resemble a kind of 'old curiosity shop' of the monarchy, an eldorado of pensioners, eccentrics and writers. In reality, the decade before the turn of the century – the decade of the Omladina trial of Czech nationalist revolutionaries for subversive activities – had already seen the beginning of disputes between the Czechs and the Germans, with street battles and assassinations. The bourgeoisie tried to ignore such events, but the schoolchildren were almost impelled to take note through the 'traditional' fights between Czech and German pupils. As a boy, Oskar Baum, later a friend of Kafka's, lost his sight in one of these brawls.

Kafka's father, of course – as his son explains in his 'Letter' – was not interested in these disputes: 'You were capable, for instance, of running down the Czechs, and then the Germans and then the Jews, and what is more, not only selectively but in every respect, and finally nobody was left except yourself. For me, you took on the enigmatic quality that all tyrants have whose rights are based on their person and not on reason.' [19]

Growing up in a parental home lacking in opinions, under mysterious laws and in incomprehensible surroundings, the child cut himself off from the outside world: 'I thought only of things in the present and their present condition.' [20] It was these experiences of his own childhood that led Kafka (with a nod to Swift's satirical remarks on the subject in *Gulliver's Travels*) to advise his sister Elli to have her son educated in a boarding school. The unusually violent tone of this letter from the 40-year-old Kafka shows how he is still affected by his past:

The selfishness of parents – the authentic parental emotion – knows no bounds. Even the greatest parental love is, as far as education is concerned, more selfish than the smallest love of the paid educator. It cannot be otherwise. For parents do not stand in a free relationship to their children, as an adult stands towards a child – after all, they are his own blood, with this added grave complication: the blood of both the parents. When the father 'educates' the child (it is the same for the mother) he will, for example, find things in the child that he already hates in himself and could not overcome, since the weak child seems to be more in his power than he himself. And so in a blind fury, without waiting for the child's own development, he reaches into the depths of the growing human being to pluck out the offending element. Or he realises with horror that something which he regards as his own distinction and which, therefore, (therefore!) should not be lacking from the family (the family!) is lacking in the child and so he begins to pound it into the child. Which effort is successful, but at the same time disastrous, for in the process he pounds the child to pieces ... He sees in the child only the thing he loves, he clings to that, he makes himself its slave, he consumes it out of love.

This tyranny or slavery, born of selfishness, are the two educational methods of parents, all gradations of tyranny or slavery. Tyranny can express itself as great tenderness ('You must believe me, since I am your mother') and slavery can express itself as pride ('You are my son, so I will make you into my saviour'). But these are two frightful educational methods, and likely to trample the child back into the ground from which it came.[21]

This passage is a thinly disguised description of Kafka's own 'upbringing'. Even in later life he was still trying to live up to the ideal 'drummed into him' by his father. When he was already a civil servant he apprenticed himself to a gardener, and subsequently to a carpenter. Time and again he admired the business efficiency of superiors or the energy, determination and assurance of friends (how often did he say or write this to his best friend Max Brod, who seemed to him a model in this respect?), and he admired mere physical robustness, such as that of the furniture removers whom he watched in Berlin six months before his death. Admittedly, this attitude was enhanced by a strong sense of justice (inherited from his mother) which eventually, in connection with his progressive loneliness, led to something very much like an idolatry of purity, reflected also in such side effects as his vegetarian lifestyle and his inclination towards naturopathy – while at the same time, Kafka joined the avant-garde of an important reform movement.

3

What does a Boy Learn at an Imperial and Royal Secondary School?

KAFKA'S LONELINESS, his mysterious isolation in an environment as rich in opportunities for contact as Prague, was due mainly to his pragmatic and abstract education. This is not necessarily a reproach against his parental home. This child, more than most, would have required a degree of empathy for which not only his father lacked the time and the education, but for which the society of his day lacked all understanding. Typical in this respect was the humanist *Gymnasium* (secondary school) to which Kafka was entrusted at the age of ten. It was housed in the Kinsky Palace, a Baroque building on *Altstädter Ring* (Staroměstské náměstí), only a few steps from where the family lived. This time, Kafka's father had made a deliberate choice – not simply a German school again, but the *Gymnasium* from which the monarchy customarily recruited its civil servants.

The outward dignity of the building on the *Altstädter Ring* was an accurate reflection of the spirit of the institution. School regulations going back several decades made any contact between teacher and pupil virtually impossible; they demanded respect and promoted an atmosphere of mindless cramming that was indifferent to the pupil's personal interests. At the end of the year, the institution published

The Kinsky Palace housed both the *Gymnasium* Kafka attended
and, on the street front, the premises of his father's shop.

a report. In one of these, Kafka's form master, Emil Gschwind (by
the standards of the day quite a liberal pedagogue), writes about the
'work syllabus, laid down for the whole year', explains the use of a
'textbook of grammatical model sentences', and ends by stating that
these are aimed chiefly at pupils 'who bring with them from home
the art of storytelling'.

The Viennese satirist Karl Kraus (1874–1936) gave the following wry, if somewhat exaggerated, account of the deadening effect
of education in the Habsburg Empire: 'The greater the quantity
of associative material supplied by the system, the less able pupils
were to assimilate it. The material the school provided you with was
supplied to furnish you with all you needed.' Yet the educational
machine through which Kafka was pushed for eight years scarcely

provided even the bare minimum of associative material: nearly half the teaching time was devoted to Latin and Greek; history was basically confined to antiquity; the teaching of German consisted of a primer course of three periods a week; modern foreign languages, music, art and physical education were optional. Even 20 years later, the Austrian philosopher Fritz Mauthner (1849–1923) could sneer at his 'humanistic' education:

> The cardinal mistake, it still seems to me today [1917], was the profound mendacity of the system, an obvious gulf between school programmes and school performance ... In the school programme ... it was always asserted that by studying Latin and Greek one would be introduced to the spirit of the ancient world. And even a modern education, it was argued, could not be acquired without that spirit ... Maybe the best philologists penetrate a little into the spirit of antiquity during their years at university. Among us pupils – there were about 40 of us in our form – only three or four got so far that, with great difficulty, they managed to translate an ancient classical writer word for word; nor did these chosen ones lack the stereotyped enthusiasm for Homer or Sophocles. But any understanding of the special quality, of the incomparable and inimitable nature, and hence also of the strangeness of the spirit of antiquity – that was totally absent. And the rest of the pupils, nine-tenths of the form, passed the school leaving exam with good success, although they had never seen in the ancient languages anything but a scourge. They derived neither pleasure nor use from the ancient languages and only learned a smattering which they forgot immediately after their exam.[1]

To Kafka, too, the 'spirit of antiquity' remained alien; very rarely does even the name of an ancient author appear in his diaries or letters. The two hours a day of Greek and Latin literature drill were predominantly an excuse for a grammatical paperchase. And cultural history (as yet untouched by the seminal Swiss historian of Renaissance culture, Jacob Burckhardt) was taught as an untroubled joyous feast, in line with the German poet Schiller's* 'Gods of Greece': 'Better creatures, nobler figures ... more heroic, more divine their virtue ... Beauteous images, serene and cheerful even in the face of need.'[2]

How was an impartial student to reconcile this artificial picture of history with events in the world around him? There was no opportunity for comparing existing social and political conditions with those of the past. Admittedly, this became one of the preconditions of Kafka's 'critique': because there was no opportunity for comparison, he viewed the society of his own day in perhaps a more abstract manner but with an unforgiving clarity.

The teaching of German was virtually worthless, aimed as it was at learning by rote and reeling off quotations. Lessons were based on bowdlerised school-edition anthologies of excerpts from writers with a cosy *Biedermeier* outlook. Their staple bill of fare comprised long-since forgotten minor authors like Halm, Gilm, Bodenstedt, Lingg, Greif and Baumbach. The only positive, albeit strongly tendentious, feature of these primers was their extensive use of Goethe.[†]

---

*German dramatist and poet Friedrich von Schiller (1759–1805) began his career as a member of the *Sturm und Drang* (Storm and Stress) group, with dramas of social and political revolt such as *The Robbers* (*Die Räuber*, 1781), and *Cabal and Love* (*Kabale und Liebe*, 1784). He is best known for his play *Don Carlos* (1787) and his poem 'Ode to Joy' ('An die Freude', c.1788), set to music by Ludwig van Beethoven. He also wrote the trilogy *Wallenstein* (1796–9), the greatest historical drama in the German language. This was followed by *Mary Stuart* (*Maria Stuart*, 1800), *The Maid of Orleans* (*Die Jungfrau von Orleans*, 1801), and *William Tell* (*Wilhelm Tell*, 1804), a dramatic manifesto for political freedom.

†The great German poet and dramatist Johann Wolfgang von Goethe

On the fourth page there was invariably a 'canon of poetic texts to be memorised'; pupils of the fifth form, for instance, were prescribed 470 lines of verse. From Goethe to Emanuel Geibel, the authors of these texts were more or less irrelevant; the only purpose of poetry was for it to be set as a test.

Religious instruction was organised differently, but led to similar results. In 'Letter to his Father', Kafka writes of the 'nothing of Judaism' that had been conveyed to him:

It was indeed, so far as I could see, a mere nothing, a joke – not even a joke. Four days a year you went to the synagogue, where you were, to say the least, closer to the indifferent than to those who took it seriously, patiently went through the prayers as a formality, sometimes amazed me by being able to show me in the prayer book the passage that was being said at that moment, and for the rest, so long as I was present in the synagogue (and this was the main thing) I was allowed to hang about wherever I liked. And so, I yawned and dozed through the many hours (I don't think I was ever so bored, except later at dancing lessons) and did my best to enjoy the few little bits of variety there were, as for instance when the Ark of the Covenant was opened, which always reminded me of the shooting galleries where a cupboard door would open in the same way whenever one hit

---

(1749–1832) achieved fame with his self-revelatory novel *The Sorrows of Young Werther* (*Die Leiden des jungen Werthers*, 1774), inspired by a hopeless affair with a friend's fiancée. His artistic range was impressive, from simple love lyrics to profound philosophical poems, novels, travelogues, verse idylls, satires, comedies, tragedies, short stories and scientific treatises. After the drama *Egmont* (1787), and the novel *Elective Affinities* (*Die Wahlverwandtschaften*, 1809), he is chiefly remembered for *Faust* (1808–32). A towering influence on German literature, Goethe was buried near his friend Schiller in the ducal vault at Weimar.

Prague's
Old-New-Synagogue.

a bull's eye; except that there, something interesting always
came out and here it was always just the same old dolls without
heads ... But otherwise I was not fundamentally disturbed in my
boredom.

That's how it was in the synagogue; at home it was possibly
even poorer, being confined to the first Seder [a ritual meal,
part of Passover], which more and more developed into a farce,
with fits of hysterical laughter ... Even in this there was still
Judaism enough, but it was too little to be handed on to the
child; it all dribbled away while you were passing it on ... The
whole thing is, of course, no isolated phenomenon. It was much
the same with a large section of this transitional generation of
Jews, which had migrated from the still comparatively devout
countryside to the cities. At bottom the faith that ruled your life
consisted in your believing in the unconditional rightness of the
opinions of a certain class of Jewish society.[3]

(This last sentence, incidentally, is one of the few in which Kafka speaks of his father's mania for social recognition. There is only one other place where he is more outspoken, saying that his father 'could scarcely be shaken by religious scruples unless they were strongly mixed with social scruples'.[4])

The faith package handed down to Kafka was, therefore, exceedingly small. Even his Bar Mitzvah at 13, announced by his father as a 'Confirmation' in line with assimilated practice, was to Kafka just 'ridiculous memorising',[5] since he knew hardly any Hebrew. (Not until two decades later, did he embark on a more thorough study.) On the other hand, there were in his form some pupils from Orthodox families, who brought a command of Hebrew from their homes, with the result that Kafka probably had a similar early experience of Judaism to that recalled by Fritz Mauthner: 'Our Jewish religious instruction consisted of two unconnected halves – moralising religious tuition that was too stupid even for the stupidest among us, and a practice of Semitic philology that might have presented many a learned orientalist with some hard nuts to crack.'[6] About Bible instruction at school, Kafka later had this to say: 'The history of the Jews is given an appearance of a fairy-tale, which men can dismiss, together with their childhood, into the pit of oblivion.'[7]

During the final years at his *Gymnasium*, Kafka's rejection of anything religious grew even stronger:

> I remember that when I was at the *Gymnasium* I often ...
> argued the existence of God with Bergmann [a school friend,
> who later become a philosopher and distinguished Israeli
> academic] in a Talmudic style either my own or imitated from
> him. At the time, I liked to begin with a theme I had found in
> a Christian magazine ... in which a watch and the world and
> the watchmaker and God were compared to one another, and
> the existence of the watchmaker was supposed to prove that of

Gymnasium student.

God. In my opinion, I was able to refute this very well as far as Bergmann was concerned.[8]

The 16-year-old embraced the objectives of the anti-clerical *Freie Schule* (Free School) and, under the influence of Adolf Gottwald, his natural science teacher, he read the writings of Charles Darwin, as well as evolutionist Ernst Haeckel's recently published *Riddles of the Universe*. This was almost to be expected, since to accept the 'nothing of Judaism' unquestioningly would have run directly counter to the ethical rigour the young Kafka was developing in those years. On the other hand, the lack of any support from parents or school lent a particular importance to all these philosophical problems.

'Peace of mind', however, was not to be gained in this way. Kafka's inner insecurity – normally masked by untidy clothes and rough behaviour – manifested itself in his bland style of dress and in a reserved shyness. This is an account by a classmate:

If I am to say anything characteristic about Kafka, then it is that there was nothing conspicuous about him. [...] His dress was always clean and tidy, inconspicuous and sound, but never elegant. Generally, though, he tended to stay somewhat aloof from school activities. He wasn't in the least bit conceited, but still remained rather detached as though school was something that didn't really engage his innermost being but that just had to be dealt with diligently all the same. We were all very fond of him and respected him, but could never get quite intimate with him; there was always a thin glass wall. With his quiet, courteous, sympathetic smile he opened the world for himself, but he closed himself off to it. What has stuck in my memory is the picture of a slim, tall, youthful person who looked so quiet, who was good and courteous and who looked almost saintly, who willingly acknowledged other people's merits and yet remained somehow distant and remote.[9]

A photograph of this *Gymnasium* student shows Kafka standing, a little embarrassed, leaning against overgrown balcony railings, in a high-buttoned adult suit with waistcoat, high collar and tie, his arms extended to both sides, his slender hands intertwined with the ivy. He has a powerful nose, a small, firmly closed mouth, dark hair coming from low on his forehead, grey eyes dreamily and doubtingly directed at the observer. A 'callow creature' was what he was at the time, as he notes in his diary in 1916.[10] He could expect no guidance either from his parents or from his teachers. Kafka realised this only when he had long decided to rigorously close himself off from the outside world. On a loose sheet we find this note:

So far as my experience went, both in school and at home the aim was to erase all trace of peculiarity ... A boy, for instance, who is in the middle of reading an exciting story in the evening, will never be made to realise, merely by an argument bearing solely upon himself that he must stop reading and go to bed ... That was my peculiarity. It was suppressed by means of turning off the gas and leaving me without a light. By way of explanation they said: 'Everyone is going to bed, so you must go to bed, too.' I saw this and had to believe it, although it made no sense to me. Nobody wants to carry out so many reforms as children do. Apart from this, in a certain respect, praiseworthy oppression, still, here as almost everywhere, there remained a sting that could not be made less painful by any number of general appeals ... All I felt was the injustice done to me ... My individuality was not accorded any recognition ... There is no doubt that I did not profit from my individual qualities with that true gain which finally manifests itself as permanent self-confidence. [11]

This passage already shows the typical incongruence between the external and the internal world, the complete 'indifference of a self-sufficient but coldly imaginative child'.[12] Kafka's development towards a final self-imposed isolation begins here; it ends a dozen years later. The final decade of his life, when his major works were produced, is marked only by continual and unsuccessful attempts to break out of this already essential fixation. Kafka's life therefore links up with many great 'naïve' writers, who are especially plentiful in German literature, such as Kleist or Novalis.*

Kafka never denied the persistent significance and weight of his youth. Three years before his death he wrote to his great friend Max Brod that he was 'wandering like a child in the forests of maturity'.[13] A year later, still more candidly, he wrote to Oskar Baum that his 'education basically took place in a lonely, too cold or too hot boy's bed'.[14]

---

*Heinrich von Kleist (1777–1811) was a brilliant and mercurial character whose plays and short stories are exceptionally original and powerful. Kafka was particularly fascinated by 'Michael Kohlhaas' (1808–10), Kleist's story of abuse of power and legal wrangling, which he had read at least ten times by 1913. Kleist's writing presents an often violent world ruled by chance that challenges the ordered and rational outlook of the Enlightenment. His career was cut short at the age of 34 when he killed himself in a suicide pact with a woman who was suffering from incurable cancer. Kafka described Kleist, together with Dostoevsky, Grillparzer and Flaubert, as his true 'blood relations'. In a letter to Felice Bauer, he noted that only Dostoevsky married, and added 'perhaps Kleist, when compelled by outer and inner necessity to shoot himself on the Wannsee, was the only one to find the right solution'. (*L/Felice*, p 316.)

Novalis was the pseudonym of Friedrich von Hardenberg (1772–1801), a German poet and novelist often referred to as the 'Prophet of Romanticism'. His short life was dominated by the death of his 15-year-old fiancée Sophie von Kühn, remembered in the prose lyrics of *Hymns to the Night* (*Hymnen an die Nacht*, 1800). As well as his *Devotional Songs* (*Geistliche Lieder*, 1799), he left two unfinished philosophical novels. Obsessed by death ('Life is lived for the sake of Death'), he died from tuberculosis aged 29.

At the beginning of his development, up until that diary entry of 1913 declaring his 'wish for an unthinking reckless solitude',[15] stands the child's realisation that neither school nor parental home would tolerate individuality. Initially, the child could oppose this only by 'clinging to things in the present in their present condition'.[16] This clinging to things in the 'present condition', without which clarification further progress is impossible, already reveals Kafka's increasingly apparent ethical strictness. However, this refusal to acknowledge the situation and then move on is soon interrupted by communication with the world around him. The newness encountered by the child is not, as would be natural, accepted without contradiction, in order to be later, in maturity, absorbed systematically. Thus, we find in the diary:

> As a child I was anxious ... whenever my father spoke about 'last things' or 'ultimo'. Since I wasn't curious and since I wasn't able – even if I sometimes did ask about it – to digest the answer quickly enough with my slow thinking, and since a weakly stirring curiosity once risen to the surface is often already satisfied by a question and an answer without requiring that it understand as well, the expression 'last things' remained a disquieting mystery for me.[17]

Kafka's unusual lack of curiosity here is in itself evidence of his sensitive withdrawal from the world around him. His classmate is quite right to speak of the 'glass wall' that separated Kafka from the world. His inner world is being furnished; the outside world is seen purely as a mass of material.

There is evidence that Kafka's performance at school was certainly above average and that even his teachers held this quiet student in high regard. Kafka himself claims the very opposite:

I thought ... I shall certainly not pass the entrance exam for the
Gymnasium, but I succeeded; but now I shall certainly fail in
the first class at the *Gymnasium*; no, I did not fail, and I went
on and on succeeding. This did not produce any confidence,
however; on the contrary, I was always convinced ... that the
more I achieved, the worse the final outcome would inevitably
be. Often in my mind's eye I saw the terrible assembly of the
teachers (the *Gymnasium* is only the most integral example, but
it was the same all around me), as they would meet, when I had
passed the first class, and then in the second class, when I had
passed that, and then in the third, and so on, meeting in order
to examine this unique, outrageous case, to discover how I, the
most incapable and, in any case, the most ignorant of all, had
succeeded in creeping up so far as this class, which now, when
everybody's attention had at last been focused on me, would
of course instantly spew me out, to the jubilation of all the
righteous liberated from this nightmare.[18]

This is not some arbitrary instance of an 'examination dream'. In
fact, the student only constructs this entire tissue of lies in order to
conceal his fear – which nevertheless emerges in the revealing final
sentence – that 'everybody's attention had at last been focused on
me'. It is the terrible vision of the revenge exacted by the world that
he views as a 'heap of material'. As yet, Kafka's inner world is vulner-
able: any incursion from outside is feared. In actual fact, this construction of his 'own' world still has something artificial, something
contrived, about it:

While I was still contented I wanted to be discontented, and
with all the means that my time and tradition gave me, plunged
into discontent ... Thus, I have always been discontented, even
with my contentment. Strange how play-acting, if engaged

in systematically enough, can change into reality. Childish games (though I was well aware that they were so) marked the beginning of my intellectual decline. I deliberately cultivated a facial tic, for instance, or would walk across the Graben [Na Příkopé, a boulevard in Prague] with arms crossed behind my head. A repulsively childish but successful game.[19]

Harmless and childish indeed, compared to, for instance, the youthful escapades of Rilke, who, with white gloves, walking stick and lorgnette (or dressed as a priest), a long-stemmed iris in his hand, striding solemnly, would promenade down the same Prague boulevard.*

About this time (1897/98, at the latest) Kafka began to write. But these beginnings were made difficult not only by his 'uncertainty', but also by an age in which, as he wrote mockingly a few years later, one '"created works" if one wrote bombast; there is no worse time for a beginning'.[20] His classmates wrote Roman tragedies and 'life symphonies', which they presented in a reader's circle in which Kafka occasionally participated. But he never read anything of his own and later destroyed all of his early writings. Only at one point in his diary does he refer to such an early work – a remark proving that even then his writing was not mere 'bombast', but that, through his increasing loneliness, writing was soon to acquire the greatest importance for him, along with philosophical problems.

With what misery ... I began! What a chill pursued me all day long out of what I had written! ... Once I projected a novel in

---

*Born in Prague, the Austrian poet Rainer Maria Rilke (1875–1926) is best known for his book on the sculptor Auguste Rodin (1840–1917), his novel *The Notebooks of Malte Laurids Brigge* (*Die Aufzeichnungen des Malte Laurids Brigge*, 1910), and his books of poetry *Sonnets to Orpheus* (*Die Sonnette an Orpheus*, 1923), and the *Duino Elegies* (*Duineser Elegien*, 1923).

which two brothers fought each other, one of whom went to
America while the other remained in a European prison ... So,
once I wrote down something about my prison on a Sunday
afternoon when we were visiting my grandparents ... It was
chiefly the corridor of the prison that was described in a few
lines, above all its silence and coldness; a sympathetic word
was also said about the brother who was left behind, because
he was the good brother. Perhaps I had a momentary feeling of
the worthlessness of my description, but before that afternoon
I never paid much attention to such feelings when among
relatives to whom I was accustomed (my timidity was so great
that the accustomed was enough to make me half-way happy), I
sat at the round table in the familiar room and could not forget
that I was young and called to great things out of this present
tranquillity. An uncle who liked to make fun of people finally
took the page that I was holding only weakly, looked at it briefly,
handed it back to me, even without laughing, and only said to
the others who were following him with their eyes, 'The usual
stuff.' To me he said nothing. To be sure, I remained seated and
bent as before over the now useless page of mine, but with one
thrust I had in fact been banished from society, the judgement
of my uncle repeated itself in me with what amounted almost to
real significance. And even within the feeling of belonging to a
family I got an insight into the cold space of our world which I
had tried to warm with a fire that first I wanted to seek out.[21]

This initially playful isolation is already infecting Kafka's relationship with his family: 'play-acting, if engaged in systematically
enough, can change into reality.'[22]

'The solitary centre in a solitary circle' (a phrase from Kleist's
'Sensations when Viewing Caspar David Friedrich's Seascape')
describes well the young Kafka's position with regard to the world

around him (though in his case it was still a very fluid, insecure position). His search for 'a fire to warm the cold space of our world continues'. All too often this is no more than an attempt to break out, a concealed yearning for fellowship.

Probably the most important of these attempts was the 16-year-old's turn to socialism, a turn that was not to be reversed in his later life, even though this was a very personal 'socialism', one of immediate solidarity. Thus, an octavo notebook dating from 1918 still contains a draft of a programme for a *'Brotherhood of Workers without Property'*,[23] which has wrongly been described as 'standing quite isolated in Kafka's work'. Kafka's participation in the meetings of the anarchist *Klub mladých* (Young People's Club), his reading of works by radicals such as Herzen, Kropotkin and Bezruč, and numerous other remarks offer further evidence.* (In any event, Kafka was not cut out to be a patriot: he found nothing to say in the written part of his school-leaving exam on the question 'What advantages does Austria derive from its position in the world and its soil conditions?'.) His first introduction to socialism came from his classmate, the Czech Rudolf Illowý. A future Social Democrat and publisher

---

*Russian political philosopher Alexander Ivanovich Herzen (1812–70) was imprisoned in 1834 for his revolutionary socialism and exiled to the provinces. In 1847 he left Russia for Paris, then London. His novel *Whose Fault?* (*Kto vinovat?*, 1847) attacked outmoded bourgeois morality, and his journal *The Bell* (*Kolokol*, 1857–67) was smuggled into Russia, preparing the way for the emancipation of the serfs (1861). Herzen's memoirs are regarded as his finest achievement.

Peter Kropotkin (1842–1921) was a Russian anarchist, geographer and explorer. He was imprisoned for favouring the political action of a working men's association, but escaped to England. He returned to Russia in 1917.

Petr Bezruč was the pseudonym of Vladimir Vašek (1867–1958). He became a recluse after a failed love affair and began sending anonymous political poems to a Czech magazine, posing as a miner. Eighty of these poems were published as a collection.

of social poetry, Illowý was forced to leave the *Gymnasium* for unexplained reasons, with the result that Kafka became the only socialist in his form, displaying his convictions – contrary to his usual shyness – with the traditional *rote Nelke* (red carnation).

Perhaps this was motivated more by a hidden yearning for fellowship than as a demonstration of his politics, though one should not interpret this as a lack of conviction: in situations provoked from outside, even the schoolboy Kafka displayed exceptional courage. For instance, the older schoolboys were accepted *en bloc* into a German nationalist pre-university students' association, the *Altstädter Kollegentag*. At one of its meetings on a bank of the *Moldau* (Vltava) river, it was decided to sing the *Watch on the Rhine*, which, according to nationalist custom, had to be done standing up. Kafka protested silently by remaining seated – with the result that he was thrown out immediately.

A further reflection of the school-leaver's secret yearning for fellowship was his longing for friendship, admittedly desired with such radical intensity that its fulfilment remained unlikely. In one of his earliest letters, written to his friend Oskar Pollak two years after leaving school (1903), he noted: 'People are tied together by ropes, and it's bad enough when the ropes around an individual loosen and he drops somewhat lower than the others into empty space; ghastly when the ropes break and he falls. That's why we should cling to others.'[24]

Friendship was to provide some contact, already greatly disturbed, with the outside world. During the final time at the *Gymnasium* and Kafka's first two years at university, this was to be the task of Pollak, the most mature young man in his form, of most resolute character, temperamental, an exuberant talker with interests in art history and natural history far beyond his years. It is evident that Pollak took a shine to his shy and reticent classmate, who reciprocated with a warmth that he would never achieve again. Without

Gymnasium
graduate, 1901.

doubt, Pollak was the leading partner in this friendship. Kafka even gave him manuscripts to judge – in later years he would, at most, read aloud his writing, without ever asking for an opinion. At a time of advancing isolation and great insecurity, the 18-year-old Kafka needed friendship more than he would in later life. During his university years, when Pollak was beginning to detach himself from him, Kafka wrote: 'I have really only spoken with you alone, among all the young people, and when I did talk to others it was only incidental or for your sake or through you or in reference to you. For me, you were, along with much else, also something like a window through which I could see the streets. I could not do that by myself.' [25]

The same metaphor of a window appears in an early prose sketch,

'The Street Window': 'Anyone who leads a solitary life and yet now and then wants to attach himself somewhere, whoever ... wishes to see any arm at all to which he might cling – he will not be able to manage for long without a window looking on to the street.' [26] No doubt the friendship suffered under this constellation: what is sought is just *any arm at all*. It is in this sense that we should understand the 'oratory exercise' for his German lesson, for which Kafka chose as the subject: 'How should we understand the conclusion of Goethe's *Tasso*?' Kafka had very personal reasons for his choice, for Tasso, 'rejected as a beggar and banished', says to Antonio at the end of the play:

I reach out to you with open arms,
Just as the sailor clings fast to the very
Rock upon which his vessel should have foundered.[27]

4

University, Society and Language in the Capital of Bohemia

KAFKA TOOK HIS SCHOOL-LEAVING EXAM in July 1901, and (with his Uncle Siegfried) spent a few weeks on the North Sea islands of Norderney and Heligoland. Although he was sceptical about his freedom after the hopeless constraint of the *Gymnasium*, he decided to make the most of it. At the time of his school-leaving exam, Kafka still gave philosophy as his 'chosen profession'– a plan that his father was certain to oppose. So, along with Oskar Pollak (and certainly under his influence), he began by studying chemistry, but after just two weeks switched to the 'desired' faculty of law. The dreary lectures he had to attend on the 'institution of Roman law' were scarcely designed to arouse his interest and so, in the summer, Kafka switched subjects once more to study the history of art (Dutch painting, Christian sculpture) and, more importantly, German literature under August Sauer.

Sauer, an important scholar, was then playing a major role in the conflict between Czechs and Germans. In particular, he was editor of the monthly magazine *Deutsche Arbeit* ('German Labour'), which trumpeted to the Czech population the 'cultural achievements of the Germans of Bohemia' (in the words of the journal's subtitle). Sauer, who taught the Viennese literary historian Joseph Nadler, had long been a staunch champion of the theory which held that literature was strongly influenced by its ethnic and national origins. All the arguments over the influence of nations and ethnicities were alien to Kafka: the letters he wrote to Oskar Pollak at the time contain sharp attacks on Sauer. In any case, he did not wish to continue his German studies in Prague and for a while he considered attending Munich University, actually visiting the city for a few days. The reasons why this plan was dropped are not clear. Perhaps Kafka's reluctance to mix his work and his vocation played a part, but his father's refusal to provide money for such 'useless' experiments is a more likely reason.*

Kafka, therefore, remained in Prague and in the winter term of 1902 resumed his law studies. These engendered 'detachment' and, as Kafka wrote, merely required 'that in the few months before the exams, and in a way that told severely on my nerves, I was positively living, in an intellectual sense, on sawdust which had, moreover, already been chewed for me in thousands of other people's mouths.'[1] During the boring lectures on 'Roman Civil Law', 'Pandects ii', 'Law of Obligations', 'Distrainment of Real Estate', and so on, Kafka doodled in the margins of the lecture notes.

With his law studies, Kafka's debt to his parents seemed redeemed. Kafka only attended the prescribed lectures and took his degree

---

*What his governess had to say about Kafka, the student: 'The young master was tall, slender, of a serious disposition, not very talkative. He spoke in a calm, soft voice. He mostly wore dark suits and sometimes a small black bowler hat … The young master was very hard-working. When he was at home he nearly always sat at his desk, studying and writing … Both I and the cook Fanny were always glad when Franz came to us in the kitchen. The young gentleman was not keen on cheap smiles or chatter. Even his joyful glance was, in a way, serious at the same time. He would ask us how we felt and whether we had a lot of work. Fanny sometimes complained that the master had scolded her. Franz merely nodded his head, but there was more understanding in it for the domestic staff than on the part of any of the rest of the family.' ANNA POUZAROVÁ

Uncle Siegfried Löwy, country physician in *Triesch*.

after the required minimum of eight terms. This provided him with a degree of freedom for everything else. During these years, Kafka came to know the world around him in the correct proportions. His school friend Ewald Příbram – whose father Otto was chairman of the board of directors of the Workers' Accident Insurance Institute (*Arbeiter-Unfall-Versicherungs-Anstalt*), where Kafka later worked – introduced him to that upper class of industrialists, professors and the higher nobility that would otherwise have been barred to him. For his holidays, he went regularly to the country, frequently to relatives, to *Liboch* or *Strakonitz* (Strakonice), but mostly to *Triesch* (Třešt), a village in Moravia, where his Uncle Siegfried – whom he venerated to the end of his life and whose opinions and world he perpetuated in his story 'A Country Doctor' – worked as a country physician. From one such visit, he wrote to Max Brod:

> I am riding around on the motorbike a good deal, swimming a lot, lying nude in the grass by the pond, hanging about the park until midnight with a bothersomely infatuated girl, have already tedded hay in the meadow, have set up a merry-go-round, helped trees after a storm, taken cows and goats to pasture and driven them home in the evening, played a lot of billiards, taken long walks.[2]

During term, he regularly attended performances at both the Czech and German Theatres (just as Prague's university was divided into a Czech and a German university, so there were different theatres for each language) and lectures and poetry readings organised by the Reading and Lecture Group of German Students. It was there that Kafka made the acquaintance of Max Brod, who gave a talk on Schopenhauer in October 1902 in which he called Nietzsche a 'fraud'. 'After this paper,' Brod reports,

> Kafka, who was a year older, saw me home. He used to take part in every meeting ... but until then we had hardly taken any notice of each other. It would indeed have been difficult to notice him because he so seldom opened his mouth, and because his outward appearance was above all deeply unobtrusive ... But that evening ... he was more communicative than usual. Anyhow, the endless conversation that went on while he was seeing me home began with a strong protest against my crude way of putting things.'[3]

Kafka's liking and reading of Nietzsche goes back to Oskar Pollak and especially the *Kunstwart*. This fortnightly magazine co-founded by Nietzsche, to which Kafka had subscribed during his final year at school, had a considerable influence at the time, especially on young people. Its pugnacious publisher Ferdinand Avenarius, Richard Wagner's nephew by marriage, championed, as he called it, 'chaste spontaneity' against the literary and artistic journalese of recent decades. In these polemics, nature and folklore were the principal starting points: 'Artist, be thou genuine, profound and close to nature!' Writers were told to praise the 'peasant cottage' and maintain a 'Germanic closeness to the people'. But the 'genuine', unfortunately, was often simple-minded; and what should have been 'profound' succeeded only in being strident. The outward garb of this attitude was a bizarre, if well-intentioned, cult of pseudo-archaic and folksy words meant to achieve 'closeness to the people'.

It is typical of Kafka that for a few years he imitated this 'primitive magic'. The alleged (and in certain respects real) seriousness of these endeavours attracted him and so greatly delayed his liberation from this linguistic schizophrenia. He only returned to honest diction when he began to detach himself from Pollak in late 1903. By then, Pollak had failed in his role as mediator of the outer world for Kafka. The *Kunstwart* experience made Kafka even more cautious about all 'solutions' offered from outside: he scrutinised the world around him even more closely. A symptom of this is his conspicuous preference for reading diaries, biographies and letters at this time – Hebbel, Amiel, Byron, Grillparzer, Eckermann's *Conversations with Goethe*, the letters of Goethe, Grabbe and Madame du Barry, the biographies of Schopenhauer and Dostoevsky. He explains his interest in a letter to Oskar Pollak (1904):

> If you're surveying a life like that, which towers higher and
> higher without a gap, so high you can scarcely reach it with your
> field glasses, your conscience cannot settle down. But it's good
> when your conscience receives big wounds, because that makes

it more sensitive to every twinge. I think we ought to read only the kind of books that wound and stab us. If the book we're reading doesn't wake us up with a blow on the head, what are we reading it for? So that it will make us happy, as you write? Good Lord, we would be happy precisely if we had no books, and the kind of books that make us happy are the kind we would write ourselves if we had to. But we need the books that affect us like a disaster, that grieve us deeply, like the death of someone we loved more than ourselves, like being banished into forests far from everyone, like a suicide. A book must be the axe for the frozen sea inside us.[4]

A man of barely 20 speaks here, with shocking matter-of-factness, of 'a frozen sea inside us', though at the same time he mentions the axe that is to cleave it. The wish for a more sensitive conscience and greater clarity comes through more decisively after the *Kunstwart* fog. Kafka touches upon this in his very first letter to Max Brod, of autumn 1904:

We are veritably carried by a vagrant breeze wherever it pleases, and there is a certain whimsicality to the way we clap our hands to our brows in the breeze, or try to reassure ourselves by spoken words, thin fingertips pressed to our knees. Whereas we are usually polite enough not to want to know anything about any insight into ourselves, we now weaken to some extent and go seeking it.[5]

In Kafka's earliest extant work, the fragmentary and hallucinatory story, 'Description of a Struggle', started at the same time, he wrote: 'I no longer want to hear scraps. Tell me everything, from beginning to end. I won't listen to less, I warn you. But I'm burning to hear the whole thing.'[6] This insistence on hearing 'the whole thing', which must be capable of instant and complete revelation, rather resembles a belief in a fairytale princess who will finally put everything right. But this desire for clarity is also, in the young Kafka, directly linked to amazement.

In the same letter to Brod he noted: 'On another day when I opened my eyes after a short afternoon sleep, still not quite certain I was alive, I heard my mother calling down from the balcony in a natural tone: "What are you up to?" A woman answered from the garden: "I'm having my teatime in the garden." I was amazed at the stalwart technique for living some people have.'[7] The whole experience seemed so significant to Kafka that he included it, almost word for word, in 'Description of a Struggle'.*

We find the same amazement at the magic of the simple in Brod's account of his first conversation with Kafka: 'He rejected anything that was planned for effect, intellectual or artificially thought up ... As an example – of what he himself liked – Kafka quoted a passage from Hofmannsthal, "the smell of damp flagstones in a hall". And he kept silent for a long while, said no more, as if this hidden, improbable thing must speak for itself.'[8] The sentence quoted by Kafka comes from Hugo von Hofmannsthal's essay 'Conversation about Poems', in which the main speaker praises the concreteness of poetry as the closest language, in all its inadequacy, can come to expressing reality. It so impressed Kafka that he included some of its sentences in 'Description of a Struggle', albeit with characteristic embellishments. Where Hofmannsthal quotes a line from the poet Stefan George, 'Ripe fruits knock upon the ground',[9] Kafka writes,

---

*Kafka's Wish to be a 'Red Indian': 'If only one were a Red Indian, instantly ready, and on the galloping horse, leaning into the air, time and again briefly trembling over the trembling ground, until one left off the spurs, for there were no spurs, until one threw away the reins, for there were no reins, and scarcely seeing the land ahead as smooth-cut meadow, already without horse's neck and horse's head.' From 'Meditation'.

'Unripe fruit struck senselessly from the trees on to the ground.'[10] It is these slightly offbeat, concrete evocations of a moment of reality that excite Kafka.

Kafka's amazement at things is rooted in his sense of their strangeness. Just as 'ultimo' was a 'disquieting mystery' to the child, so external reality often remained an 'embarrassing secret' to Kafka the student. The situation of the 'solitary centre in a solitary circle' remained unchanged: 'I have done nobody any harm, nobody has done me any harm, but nobody will help me. A pack of nobodies.'[11] (These lines from 'Description of a Struggle' were evidently important to Kafka. He reused the episode, under the title 'The Excursion into the Mountains' in his first book *Betruchtung*.) Again he refers to the strangeness of things: 'I felt so weak and unhappy that I buried my face in the ground: I could not bear the strain of seeing around me the things of the earth. I felt convinced that every movement and every thought was forced, and that one had to be on one's guard against them.'[12]

From this unbearable 'strain of seeing the things of the earth', Kafka escaped into their oddly arbitrary description. The world is viewed as a 'mass of material': objects within it are merely building blocks of a new world, which is initially, as we read in 'Description of a Struggle', a 'vast but yet unfinished landscape'. Under the reader's eyes this landscape is then furnished:

> Since I love pinewoods, I went through woods of this kind,
> and since I like gazing silently up at the stars, the stars appeared
> slowly in the sky, as is their wont ... Opposite and at some
> distance from my road, probably separated from it by a river
> as well, I caused to rise an enormously high mountain ... This
> sight, ordinary as it may be, made me so happy that I as a small
> bird rocking on a twig of those distant scrubby bushes, forgot to
> let the moon come up. It lay already behind the mountain, no
> doubt angry at the delay.[13]

This cool, detached view of strange things, this simple registration of sense data that nevertheless is coloured by amazement, is already the position from which his later works are narrated. Walter Benjamin referred to this aspect of Kafka's work (albeit without access to any material on Kafka's early years) as early as 1934: 'Kafka is relentless in his portrayal of people's attitudes. Yet his constant position is one of astonishment ... divesting human behaviour of all its traditional supports, he turns it into a base subject for endless speculation.' He creates arbitrary relations between things, as in a dream. He describes the process in the only diary entry in which he talks about deciding in his youth between dream and reality:

Many years ago, I sat one day, in a sad enough mood, on the slopes of the Laurenziberg [Petřín] ... I went over the wishes that I wanted to realise in life. I found that the most important or the most delightful was the wish to attain a view of life (and – this was necessarily bound up with it – to convince others of it in writing), in which life, while still retaining its natural full-bodied rise and fall, would simultaneously be recognised no less clearly as a nothing, a dream, a dim hovering. A beautiful wish, perhaps, if I had wished it rightly. Considered as a wish, somewhat as one were to hammer together a table with painful and methodical technical efficiency, and simultaneously do nothing at all, and not in such a way that people could say: 'Hammering a table together is nothing to him,' but rather: 'Hammering a table together is really hammering a table together to him, but at the same time it is nothing,' whereby certainly the hammering would have become still bolder, still surer, still more real and, if you will, still more senseless. But he could not wish in this fashion, for his wish was not a wish, but only a vindication of nothingness, a justification of non-entity, a touch of animation which he wanted to lend to non-entity, in which at that time he had scarcely taken his first few conscious steps, but which he already felt as his element. It was a sort of farewell that he took from the elusive world of youth; although youth had never directly deceived him, but only caused him to be deceived by the utterances of all the authorities he had around him. So is explained the necessity of his 'wish'.[14]

In fact, Kafka's wish to see life as both 'full-bodied' and at the same time as a 'dream, a dim hovering' marks his 'farewell from the illusory world of youth'. As he had shown in detaching himself from the literary ideals of *Kunstwart* magazine, Kafka had already developed the stubborn independence of judgement that would stay with him.

Kafka's late works are concerned with judgement, punishment and trial. This peculiarity of Kafka's has frequently been attributed to the influence of Kierkegaard's thinking. However, such typical works as *The Judgement* and *The Metamorphosis* were written before Kafka had read a single line of Kierkegaard; he first read him in 1913. Nevertheless, it is uncertain whether Kafka's peculiar strictness of judgement sprang from his own thinking alone.

One probable source was the philosophy of Franz Brentano. Although Brentano was by then living in semi-retirement as an Emeritus professor, three of his most important disciples – the language philosopher Anton Marty and the two future editors of Brentano's works, Oskar Kraus and Alfred Kastil – were professors in Prague, teaching his philosophy along strictly orthodox lines. Kafka attended a lecture by Marty as early as his second term and thereafter was a regular participant in the 'Louvre circle' (the Louvre was a café in Prague), an exclusive group whose discussions were almost entirely about Brentano. There is no reason to doubt the various reports that speak of Kafka's inability to follow abstract reasoning and his tendency to think in images. All the more remarkable, then,

The sanatorium in *Zuckmantel*.

that he remained part of the circle for more than four years – though this does tend to suggest that he found many of his own ideas mirrored or confirmed there.

Brentano divided psychological phenomena into three basic categories: imaginings, judgements and moods. According to his theory, which was strongly influenced by English utilitarian philosophers, decisions in favour of a 'moral behaviour recognised as correct' are based solely on judgement because imagination and mood are not adequate foundations for moral behaviour. Such autonomy of judgement required rigorous self-analysis. This idea first appears in Kafka's writings in 1904: 'We burrow through ourselves like a mole and emerge blackened and velvet-haired from our sandy underground.' [15] Kafka's situation called for self-analysis: he could find security only within himself, and this entailed a constant process of self-reflection. Accepting that rigorous judgement was the only basis for moral behaviour took rather longer. In the same letter, he wrote: 'We adorn ourselves, secretly hoping that the adornment will become our nature. And when people ask us about the life we intend to live, we form the habit, in spring, of answering with an expansive wave of the hand, which goes limp after a while, as if to say that it was ridiculously unnecessary to conjure up sure things.'[16] In Kafka's early prose many characters still have this floating, unde-cided quality, even though some (as in 'Wedding Preparations in the Country') appear to be strange 'without intending it, as though by some law'.[17] Not until 1912, in *The Judgement*, are Kafka's emphasis on self-analysis and judgement successfully brought together.

There is no doubt that Brentano's ideas influenced Kafka, particu-larly given that after university he rarely read philosophical works, so that any subsequent impressions were scarcely able to eclipse those earlier ones. Some later diary entries reveal his continuing concern with Brentano, including his terminology. A notebook entry of 1917 contains the expression 'descriptive psychology',[18] an echo of an Anton Marty lecture on 'Basic Questions of Descriptive Psychol-ogy' that Kafka had attended 15 years earlier.

Insecurity and self-analysis, the mystery of judgement and the strangeness of things, amazement, shy remoteness and a yearning for friendship – these were the world of the young law student.

The law studies that Kafka had taken upon himself, especially during the final terms, were tortuous. His delicate constitution was hardly up to the stress of cramming for exams. At the beginning of July 1905 he went to a sanatorium at *Zuckmantel* (Zlaté hory), a small town surrounded by forests and lakes. 'I am frivolous, this is my fourth week in a sanatorium in Silesia, where I mingle a great deal with people and womenfolk, and have become rather lively',[19] he wrote to Max Brod. And exactly ten years later: 'Basically I have never had that kind of intimacy with a woman, except for two cases – the time in Zuckmantel (but there she was a woman and I was a boy), and the time in Riva (but there she was half a child and I was altogether confused).'[20] Both encounters, the first in 1905 and 1906 (Kafka twice spent his holidays in *Zuckmantel*), and the other in 1913, took place far from Prague, on prolonged trips on which he was alone – and about both Kafka observed strict silence. The experience gave rise to a prose work preserved only as a fragment, 'Wedding Preparations in the Country', in which he set a shy memorial to his first love, while at the same time melancholically mocking his restricted life in Prague through his lead character Raban: 'In town one can very easily manage to go without what isn't good for one. If one does not do without it, then one has only oneself to blame for the bad consequences. One will be sorry and in this way come to see for the first time really clearly how to manage the next time.'[21]

His return to Prague was followed by terrible months preparing for the viva required for his doctorate when he virtually lived off wood flour and seriously strained his nerves. His supervisor was Alfred Weber (brother of the sociologist Max Weber), who had shortly before been called to Prague as professor. (Political economy was then still taught within the faculty of law, along with constitutional law and international law.) It is difficult to assess Weber's influence on Kafka, but he probably read some of his lecture notes and also his article on cottage industry, everyday problems that he would have to deal with in his future employment as an insurance assessor. The transcript of the exam notes that he scraped through with a bare pass, 'three out of five votes judging his performance adequate', while the candidate himself declared that it had been 'great fun, although I did not know very much'.[22] On 18 June 1906, Kafka was awarded his degree of Doctor of Law.

As for a choice of career, he felt utterly at a loss. Initially, he worked in a Prague law firm and in the autumn, still undecided, embarked on the one-year law-court practice prescribed for all civil service lawyers. Nowhere does Kafka speak about his experiences

The certificate confirming that Kafka had passed his exams.

in the courts; he merely notes that he 'accomplished nothing at all during my year of court clerking'.[23]

Kafka's choice of career was more or less a matter of indifference to him. His only condition was an occupation that, while providing him with independence from his parents, would at the same time leave him as much time as possible for writing – in short, an impossible job. Various plans followed as he neared the end of his year in the law courts – to take Spanish lessons, to study at the Export Academy in Vienna, to emigrate to South America. All that these ideas had in common was the greatest possible geographical distance from Prague. Nevertheless, with some resignation, eventually (on 1 October 1907) he accepted the offer of a 'temporary post' with the Assicurazioni Generali insurance company. He had 'some hopes of someday sitting in chairs in faraway countries, looking out of the office window at fields of sugar cane or Mohammedan cemeteries',[24] but resignation was no doubt stronger. Five years previously, Kafka had written: 'Prague doesn't let go. This old crone has claws.'[25] In another letter from this time he wrote: 'I am utterly on the downward path and – I can see far enough for that – I can't help going to the dogs. Also, I should love to escape from myself: but as that is impossible, there is only one thing I can rejoice about, and that is that I have no pity on myself and so I have at last become egoistic to that extent.'[26]

The 'greatest personal injury',[27] loneliness, was mainly the result of the Prague environment that Kafka came to know during his university years and his law-court practice. Even though in most cases he was hostile to it, this environment played a crucial part in the subject matter and the style of Kafka's prose. His unusual themes and his cool, clearly constructed, terse language, its characteristic purism – all these are unthinkable without Prague.

Fundamental to his range of themes was the insular seclusion of the Germans in Prague – an early form, perhaps, of modern alienation. Although Germans held nearly all the socially important positions, they were by then a minority of just 7 per cent. The cultural efforts of these industrialists, landowners, company directors, merchants, bankers and members of the *haute bourgeoisie* were often no more than exercises in intellectual self-reassurance. The fierce rebellion of the younger German-speaking generation was largely in protest against this phoney culture. If you wanted to be a writer, you were almost automatically opposed to it; prior to the First World War, if you encountered someone from Prague abroad, the first question you asked would be about their literary works.

The German writers showed hardly any interest in their surroundings. Few Czech authors were welcomed into the coffee-house circles where German writers established and reinforced their reputations. This meant that major talents were often overlooked. As a result, Kafka was probably the only one to have heard of Jaroslav Hašek before the First World War and the fame that *The Good Soldier Svejk* brought him (though Hašek's reputation as an unruly drinker and roustabout would hardly have recommended him in any case). Apart from Kafka, hardly any Prague-German writer had a decent command of Czech, with the result that their occasional, tentative approaches remained little more than patronising and romantic Czechophile gestures. The following verses by the young Rainer Maria Rilke, about the medieval religious reformer Jan Hus, an adopted hero of Czech nationalism, are typical:

> Towering mightier and higher
> Stands the great reformer Hus;
> Though we fear his doctrine's fire,
> Yet we bow in ever shyer
> Awe before his genius.[28]

Elsewhere Rilke gives his true opinion: the Czech poets, he says, are 'over-ripe' and the people 'still quite childish'.[29]

In these circumstances the position of the Jews was particularly difficult, as they represented a strong liberal force between the two camps. Theodor Herzl, the founder of Zionism, remarked in 1897:

> What then had they done, the little Jews of Prague, the decent merchants of Prague, the most peaceful of all peaceful citizens?

The *Altstädter Ring* with the column of the Virgin Mary.

In Prague they are accused of not being Czechs, in Saaz and Eger they are accused of not being Germans ... so where are they to stand? There are some who wanted to be German, and the Czechs pounced on them – and Germans, too ... If one considers the entirely wrong attitude of the Bohemian Jews, one understands why they are rewarded for their services with blows.

Curiously enough, the two opposing ethnic groups in Bohemia
have found a new variant to the old story of the postilions.
In this anecdote, two stagecoaches meet on a narrow track.
Neither postilion wants to give way and there is a Jew in both
coaches. So each driver cracks his whip towards the passenger in
the other coach: 'If you'll beat my Jew I'll beat your Jew!' Except
that in Bohemia you should add: 'And mine, too!' [30]

Pavel Eisner has accurately described the defensive attitude of the
Prague Jews towards the outside world as a move from a religious
into a social ghetto. They replaced religious faith with its cultural
or social derivatives, and religious ties with business connections.
The sons of this generation inherited nothing; Kafka in 'Letter to
his Father' calls himself 'in sober truth a disinherited son'.[31] The
intensity of his love-hate for his father meant that Kafka tended
to see his 'disinheritance' as his personal fate, rather than a more
general pattern of strife between generations. But he was aware of
the more general problem. Thus, he notes: 'Prague. Religions get
lost as people do.'[32] His work equally reflects this separation and
isolation in their proper proportion.

Nearly all the Prague authors deceived themselves, either know-
ingly or unknowingly, about the reality of their isolation. Kafka alone,
throughout his life, denied himself the reassurance of belonging to
a community, party or group. But without that security, Kafka had
no firm standpoint from which to gain a clear perspective on what
was happening around him – or even on his own 'scribblings'. This is
perhaps one reason why there are no assessing or commenting narra-
tors in Kafka's novels and short stories. Three years before his death,
Kafka made this resigned entry in his diary: 'I have seldom, very
seldom crossed this borderland between loneliness and fellowship,
I have even been settled there longer than in loneliness itself. What
a fine bustling place was Robinson Crusoe's island in comparison!' [33]

Kafka's contemporaries – Gustav Meyrink, Egon Erwin Kisch, Paul Leppin, Viktor Hadwiger, Max Brod, Oskar Wiener, as well as the young Werfel and Rilke – had found their island. But they rarely allowed their isolation to enter their work as a theme. Instead, their writings sought to evade the reality of their situation. Paul Leppin later admitted: 'During the last few decades there was a total lack, within the German districts of Prague, of an organic development of intellectual matters. What we have gives the impression of ready-purchased furniture, mass-produced as a lot.'[34]

The young literati sat in the Café Arco – the Viennese satirist Karl Kraus derided them as 'Arconauts' – drafting especially effective programmes for making fools of the bourgeoisie. With good justification, Werfel, in his *Embezzled Heaven*, spoke of 'those snobs who run around as mystics or orthodox Jews because all the tailors, schoolmasters and journalists are already atheists, believing in science'.[35] Bourgeois society had a point when it accused the young writers of producing works that were mystagogical, bloodthirsty, obscene and contrived. In fact, it was these qualities that made them famous at the time (and mostly indigestible today).

The forcing house atmosphere of Prague produced works of monstrous eroticism and sultry sexuality. Long before the creation of Dr Mabuse and his ilk, their world was a horrible waxworks museum in which the first 'extreme types' appear – murderers, lepers, pimps, perverts, drunkards, spectres, *doppelgänger*, obsessives, cretins, homunculi. This flight into make-believe is reflected in the language, with its perfumed verbal acrobatics, overextended metaphors and baroque adjectives.

Paul Leppin: 'Here a strident, demanding trumpet sounded a ringing fanfare somewhere in the hall. And Marta-Bianca saw Daniel Jesus and the enormous woman getting up from their seat and two mute lackeys bringing in a black crown, in which the precious stones were deathly pale like tears.'[36]

Rainer Maria Rilke: 'Her bleared eyes, that looked as though some diseased person had spat green slime under her bloody eyelids.' Or: 'Laughter bubbled from their mouths like matter from open sores.' [37]

Gustav Meyrink: 'Glittering hand-sized butterflies, strangely patterned, sat with their wings open, like open magic books, on silent flowers.' [38] (It was this passage that Kafka 'superciliously' criticised as artificial in one of his first conversations with Brod.)[39]

Nearly all the products of the 'Prague school' exhibit this dishonest and inflated style; the riches suggested by magic books, gold and precious stones are fake. The patent discrepancy between it and Kafka's prose, whose terse, cool, aloof language had been noted by his contemporaries, either critically or approvingly, stems from the specific situation of the German language in Prague, well-described by Fritz Mauthner: 'The German in the interior of Bohemia, surrounded as he is there by a Czech rural population, speaks paper German, lacking the fullness of expression rooted in the earth, lacking dialectal forms. The language is poor.' [40] Under the pressure of isolation, this 'Prague German', which many of the city's inhabitants regarded as unsurpassed in its purity, increasingly became a state-subsidised language register only used on high days and holidays. One striking aspect of this process was the dwindling vocabulary; tellingly, even in later life, Rilke would scour dictionaries in the Bibliothèque Nationale in Paris looking for exotic words. The suspiciously rich vocabulary for which Prague German was often praised in fact derived from a basic linguistic poverty. With unintended frankness, Franz Werfel described the way some of the Prague German writers became affected and verbose in their attempts to break out of their constricted linguistic shell:

That is why I praise self-satisfied dignity,
My lofty rhetoric practised in the evenings.

In 1908, Kafka published his first work in this magazine, eight prose pieces with the title *Betrachtung* ('Observation').

What shields me from suicide and evil thoughts
Are arrangement of folds, cothurnus and tragic declamation![41]

Kafka practised no rhetoric in the evenings, and so was not protected from 'suicide and evil thoughts', as Wertel would put it. Indeed, even at the time, fully in line with prevailing facts, Wertel offered the opinion: 'Nobody beyond Tetschen-Bodentach will understand Kafka'. Kafka's characteristic purism, the sober construction of his sentences and his sparse vocabulary, are unthinkable without the background of Prague German. His decision to confine himself to the limited linguistic resources of his surroundings is simple honesty – though the sheer extravagance of the *Kunstwart* style may have been a contributory factor. Kafka's sense of the 'strangeness' of things can also be linked to his linguistic background. There was always something forbidding and alien about the dry, printed-page style of Prague German, right down to the use of individual words. Taken out of their familiar context, words, metaphors and phrases regained their original semantic multiplicity, becoming richer in images and associative opportunities. In Kafka's work we find chains of association on almost every page, resulting from a strictly literal understanding of words and phrases, one image leading to another. An example from the short story 'A Country Doctor': 'Your wound is not so bad. Done in a tight corner with two strokes of the axe. Many a one proffers his side and can hardly hear the axe in the forest, far less that it is coming near him.'[42]

The 'not so bad' is followed by the image of the wound as a pure, geometric 'tight corner' (the phrase also means 'at an acute angle'), the two sides of which were done with 'two strokes of the axe'. And then the 'axe' sparks off one of those strings of associations, so typical of Kafka, which digress completely from the real chain of events.

Likewise, in the famous closing sentence of *The Trial*, rather than offer us the standard formulation 'He felt as though ...', Kafka writes 'It was as if the shame would outlive him'. This literal interpretation of language and its proverb-like associations generate the wealth of images in Kafka's prose. The literary bustle of his contemporaries on the other hand remained just as Max Brod had deplored it in his first novel: 'Sick from too much conception, from too many opportunities, incomplete, a victim of intellectual free trade.'[43]

Kafka's decision to use the basic language of his environment develops slowly from his story 'Description of a Struggle' (begun in 1904) to *The Judgement* (1912). At the beginning of this development, we still find extensive descriptions and commentary. Then the similes (used to excess by the Prague School) gradually disappear until, in the high style of his principal works, he relies, to an almost dangerous degree, on the power of the individual word. Description and commentary are dispensed with. Instead, Kafka's prose challenges others to provide a commentary on it – with sometimes unfortunate results.

Kafka was entirely aware of the political and social position of the Germans in Prague. In a letter, he observes tersely: 'I have never lived among German people.'[44] Whether he also understood the linguistic prerequisites of this position is not entirely certain. In any case, such a realisation would not have affected the young Kafka's decision in favour of clarity of language, which came of its own accord. This curious decision – in favour of the language of his generation but against its writers – certainly had psychological causes, too: Kafka could at least emancipate himself from his milieu in a way he never could from his parents. In his diary, he wrote: 'I, who for the most part have been a dependent creature, have an infinite yearning for independence and freedom in all things. Rather put on blinkers and go my way to the limit than have the familiar pack mill around me and distract my gaze.' [45]

5

'Description of a Struggle': the Insurance Official, his Job, his Plans and his Journeys

IN OCTOBER/NOVEMBER 1907, a year after graduating as a Doctor of Law and a few days after finally deciding on a career, the 24-year-old Kafka wrote:

> My life is completely chaotic now. At any rate, I have a job with a tiny salary of 80 crowns and an immense eight to nine hours of work; but I devour the hours outside the office like a wild beast. Since I was not previously accustomed to limiting my private life to six hours, and since I am also studying Italian and want to spend the evenings of these lovely days out of doors, I emerge from the crowdedness of my leisure hours scarcely rested ...
>
> I am in the Assicurazioni Generali and have some hopes of someday sitting in chairs in faraway countries, looking out of the office windows at fields of sugar cane or Mohammedan cemeteries; and the whole world of insurance itself interests me greatly, but my present work is dreary ...
>
> I don't complain about the work so much as about the sluggishness of swampy time. The office hours, you see, cannot be divided up; even in the last half hour I feel the pressure of the eight hours just as much as in the first. Often it is like a train ride

lasting night and day, until in the end you're totally crushed; you no longer think about the straining of the engine, or about the hilly or flat countryside, but ascribe all that's happening to your watch alone, which you continually hold in your palm ... All people in this sort of work are like that. The springboard for their cheerfulness is the last moment in the office.

I have no stories, see no people; for my daily walk I scurry down four alleyways whose corners I have already rounded off, and across a square. I'm too tired for plans. Perhaps I'll gradually turn to wood from my ... fingertips on up ... But it isn't laziness alone, it's also fear, generalised fear of writing, of this horrible pursuit; yet all my unhappiness now is due to my being deprived of it.[1]

The 'pressure' of the office hours, the staring at his watch, to which 'all that's happening' is ascribed, the last moment in the office as the 'springboard for cheerfulness' – the same metaphors appear years later in a letter and they were the fundamental aspect under which Kafka saw his daily work. Admittedly, the working regulations in this private insurance company were especially strict. The staff were obliged, 'whenever the company requires it, to work also at unusual hours without a claim to special remuneration'; they were not permitted to 'accept any office or honorary office without the written consent of th management, which might be withdrawn by it at any moment'. In return, the management was prepared, 'at the request of the employee, to grant him a fortnight's vacation every other year ... the timing [of such] a vacation being determined by the management in the light of the requirements of his work'.

Tellingly, Kafka readily accepted these rigorous conditions, not only because of his ever stronger desire to leave Prague, 'that damned city'[2] (as he had called it in a letter a few months previously), for those chairs in faraway countries, but also because of his wish to

Felix Weltsch.

be independent of his parents. That was the reason why he entered employment with the Assicurazioni Generali on the very day after completing his year's practice in the law courts. It was at the insurance company that duty and inclination clashed for the first time: 'Immediate contact with the workaday world deprives me – though inwardly I am as detached as I can be – of the possibility of taking a broad view of matters, just as if I were at the bottom of a ravine, with my head bowed down in addition.'[3] Such a 'broad view', which Kafka was to acquire only in his last years, was here in danger of being lost as he began again to communicate with the outer world, albeit only through the 'window' of friendship.

Following the breakdown of Kafka's relationship with Oskar Pollak, it was Max Brod who linked Kafka to the outer world during his early years of employment.* Through him Kafka came to know

---

*Max Brod: Kafka's lifelong friend, his first editor and biographer, was born in Prague in 1884. A qualified lawyer, he worked for a long time in the financial and postal administration. He began to write at an early age, as a novelist and a

the area around Prague, and together they went on holiday to northern Italy, Weimar, Paris and Switzerland. Brod accompanied Kafka to Prague's nightclubs, bars and coffee houses and introduced him to the city's literary life – in which he himself had always participated much more than Kafka. Brod introduced him to friends of Kafka's age – the courteous and ironic philosopher and Zionist Felix Weltsch and the more reticent blind writer Oskar Baum (both of whom became lifelong friends of Kafka). Brod encouraged Kafka, despite the latter's hesitations, to read his work to this circle of friends, urged him to write more, supported the publication of his writings, and prevented him from becoming isolated from the world about him. Brod recognised his friend's talent before anyone else. But he was also attracted by Kafka's personality:

> He had an unusual aura of power about him, such as I have
> never met anywhere else, even when I met very important
> famous men ... He never spoke a meaningless word. Everything
> that came from him came in a way that became less and less
> forced as the years went on, a precious expression of his quite
> special way of looking at things – patient, life-loving, ironically
> considerate towards the follies of the world and, therefore,
> full of sad humour. But never forgetful of the real kernel, 'The
> Indestructible', and so, always far from being blasé or cynical ...
> In his presence the everyday world underwent a transformation,
> everything was new, new in a way that was often very sad, not
> to say shattering ... In addition, it was not only on me but on
> many others that Kafka had the effect I have described. No one
> at that time beyond myself knew his literary work. There was no

theatre and music critic. Generous to people more talented than himself, Brod promoted not only Kafka, but also Leos Janáček and many others. In 1913 he became a Zionist and in 1939 emigrated to Palestine, where he worked as drama director at the Habimah theatre. He died in Tel Aviv in 1968.

need of his works, the man produced his own effect himself, and despite all the shyness of his behaviour, he was always quickly recognised by men of worth as someone out of the ordinary.[4]

For his part, Kafka, as he noted in his diary in 1911, was 'almost entirely under Max's influence', and admired not only his 'energy',[5] but also his (to Kafka, incomprehensible) literary productivity, his skill at dealing with people, his ceaseless activity. As early as 1907, Kafka wrote to him: 'You need a great deal of activity. I am sure about your requirements in this respect, even though I cannot comprehend them.'[6] He evidently admired Brod's selflessness and modesty just as much, as reported by Stefan Zweig:

I still see him as I saw him for the first time – a young man of 20, small, slightly built and of infinite modesty ... He talks of music, of Smetana and Janáček, whom he discovered for the world, but always about others, never about himself or his own songs and sonatas. One asks him about his work: instead of an answer, he praises a totally unknown Franz Kafka as the real master of modern prose and psychology. One asks about his poetry, but he waves this away: on a school bench, he says, sits a man by name of Franz Werfel who is one of the greatest lyrical poets of our day. This is what he was like then, this young poet, totally devoted to everything that seemed great to him ...[7]

There is no doubt that Brod's activity at times seemed as strange to Kafka as the hustle and bustle of the external world. In 'Wedding Preparations in the Country', written while he was deciding on his career, he questions the event-filled outside world with something like the playfulness 'of a child in matters that are dangerous'. In this story 'one' ('*Man*') and 'I' ('*Ich*') are split. Only 'one' (the public self) takes part in the world, only the body is sent to the wedding

Max Brod.

preparations in the country; the 'I', transformed into a beetle, stays at home. The motif of Kafka's most famous story, *The Metamorphosis*, is anticipated, six years earlier:

> One works so feverishly at the office that afterwards one is too tired even to enjoy one's holiday properly. But even all that work does not give one a claim to be treated lovingly by everyone; on the contrary, one is alone, a total stranger. And so long as you say 'one' instead of 'I', there's nothing in it and one can easily tell the story; but as soon as you admit to yourself that it is you yourself, you feel as though transfixed and are horrified ... But if I myself distinguish between 'one' and 'I' how then dare I complain about the others? Probably they're not unjust, but I'm too tired to take it all in ...
>
> All the people who try to torment me, and who have now occupied the entire space around me, will quite gradually be thrust back by the beneficent passage of these days, without my

having to help them even in the very least. And, as it will come about quite naturally, I can be weak and quiet and let everything happen to me, and yet everything must turn out well, through the sheer fact of the passing of the days.

And besides, can't I do it the way I always used to as a child in matters that were dangerous? I don't even need to go to the country myself, it isn't necessary. I'll send my clothed body. If it staggers out of the door of my room, the staggering will indicate not fear but its nothingness. Nor is it a sign of excitement if it stumbles on the stairs, if it travels into the country, sobbing as it goes, and there eats its supper in tears. For I myself am meanwhile lying in my bed, smoothly covered over with the yellow-brown blanket, exposed to the breeze that is wafted through the seldom-aired room.

As I lie in bed I assume the shape of a big beetle, a stag beetle or a cockchafer, I think ...

The form of a large beetle, yes. Then I would pretend it was a matter of hibernating, and I would press my little legs to my bulging belly. And I would whisper a few words, instructions to my sad body, which stands close beside me, bent. Soon I shall have done – it bows, it goes swiftly, and it will manage everything efficiently while I rest.[8]

The 'horror at being strange' and only 'an object of curiosity' is the same schoolboy nightmare of his teachers suddenly meeting to examine his 'outrageous' case and focusing 'general attention' on it. It is the fear of the outer world bursting into the inner world, here held in check by dispatching only the 'clothed body'. In *The Metamorphosis* there is no longer this concession. In 1913, Kafka notes in his diary, with some satisfaction, the final stage of this development: 'In me, by myself without human relationship, there are no visible lies. The limited circle is pure.'[9]

First edition of *Die Verwandlung* (*The Metamorphosis*), published in Leipzig, Germany, in 1916.

During his stressful work at the Assicurazioni Generali his writing stopped altogether, which was the reason why, from within a few months of his joining the firm, he began to look for another position. After nine months, Kafka left the company and two weeks later, in July 1908, joined the Workers' Accident Insurance Institute for the Kingdom of Bohemia in Prague (*Arbeiter-Unfall-Versicherungs-Anstalt für das Königreich Böhmen in Prag*), where he worked until his retirement in 1922. The Insurance Institute was a semi-governmental body which dealt with the insurance of workers against industrial accidents and conducted inspections of factories to ensure that they complied with safety standards. Working conditions there were vastly better and, most importantly, office hours ended at two o'clock in the afternoon, so that his hours, including regular overtime and working six days a week, were in line with modern practice. Before Kafka joined the staff, the Insurance

Institute was one of those establishments, common in the old Austria-Hungary, where bureaucracy and slackness were inextricably mingled. That it had been making a loss for the previous 15 years suggests as much. Not until 1908 was a new director appointed, and it was in connection with this new regime that Kafka was enrolled as a lawyer in the Insurance Institute initially as a 'temporary civil servant', then from 1910 as 'Concipist' [a kind of drafting clerk] with civil service status. His 'service record' shows that in 1913 he was appointed a 'Vice Secretary', in 1920 an 'Institution Secretary', and in 1922 a 'Senior Secretary'. His early retirement followed shortly afterwards, on 1 July 1922.

Among the predominantly Czech staff, Kafka – the 'office child' – was extremely popular: 'He didn't have a single enemy.' [10] People asked him for advice or help. One of his colleagues reports: 'Kafka used to dictate his drafts to an employee for typing. This employee frequently found himself, guiltlessly, in financial difficulties. What was more natural than that he should ask Kafka for small short-term loans – and these were never refused. But Kafka invariably declined to accept repayment with the remark: "You need the help, and I am able to provide it."' [11]

Kafka was soon recognised as – in the words of his superior – an 'excellent drafting clerk'.[12] A number of his contributions to the Institute's annual reports have survived, providing us with an accurate idea of his area of work – chiefly the processing of employers' appeals against the assignment of their firms to particular risk categories, legal information for enterprises, and measures for the prevention of accidents. The Institute's efforts to reform itself encountered opposition from all sides, opposition which Kafka worked to overcome not only in his contributions to the annual reports, but also in articles for the daily press, published under pseudonyms. Employers, even 'large enterprises that have to be informed on basic questions of insurance,'[13] were forever trying 'maliciously to withhold' their

The Workers' Accident Insurance Institute. Kafka worked there from 1908 to 1922. His office was on the fourth floor.

mandatory contributions. The 'workers, whose vital interests were here threatened, showed indifference'.[14] The representative bodies of the employers opposed compulsory insurance on principle so that 'the question often became entangled with issues removed from the matter itself [which they] did not understand properly, [of which] they were unable to grasp the technical detail and, therefore, given the multitude of conflicting interests which they had to represent, chose the solution that seemed at the time the most convenient and, thus, the easiest to understand.' [15]

The fate of the workers in these circumstances became especially clear to Kafka through processing accident compensations and in his work promoting accident prevention, another duty assigned to him. (The compensation payments averaged 1,000 crowns, about a year's wages.) A passage from an article on safety by Kafka, championing the introduction of round safety rollers in wood planing machines runs:

Our illustrations show the difference between square spindles and cylindrical spindles as it affects the technique for the prevention of accidents. The cutters of the square spindle (Figure 1), are connected by means of screws directly to the spindle and rotate with exposed cutting edges at speeds of 3,800 to 4,000 revolutions per minute. The dangers to the operator, presented by the large space between the cutter spindle and the surface of the table are obvious. Such spindles were used either because the danger was not realised, which may incidentally have increased the danger, or with the knowledge of the presence of a permanent danger which could not be avoided. Although an extremely cautious operator could take care not to allow any joint of his fingers to project from the timber when guiding it over the cutter head, the main danger defied all caution. The hand of even the most cautious operator was bound to be drawn into the cutter space if it slipped, particularly when, as often happened, the timber was hurled back (by the cutter block) while the operator was pressing the article to be planed against the table with one hand and feeding it to the cutter spindle with the other. This lifting and recoiling of the timber could not be anticipated or prevented as it may have been due to gnarls or knots in the timber, to an insufficiently high cutting-speed, to warped cutters, or to uneven pressure of the operator's hands on the article. In such accidents usually several joints, and even whole fingers, were severed (Figure 2). Not only every precaution but also all protecting devices seemed to fail in the face of this danger, as they either proved to be totally inadequate or, whereas they reduced the danger on the one hand (automatic covering of the cutter slot by a protective slide, or by reducing the width of the cutter space), they increased it on the other by not allowing the chippings sufficient space to leave the machine, which resulted in choked cutter spaces and in injured fingers when the operator attempted to clear the slot of chippings.

This square spindle is juxtaposed in Figure 3 ... to a safety spindle.

The blades of this roller are completely protected, embedded as they are between the flap ... or between a cone and the massive body of the roller ...

This device reduces the overwhelming likelihood of fingers becoming trapped in the cutter space. Where this does occur, however, the injuries will be superficial cuts and abrasions (Figure 4) and will not interrupt the work process.[16]

Reform of the Insurance Institute and the introduction of measures to prevent accidents progressed slowly. Over the years, Kafka had, time and again, to examine cases of workmen injured or crippled by inadequate machines. He became gradually more sceptical of the Institute. Though he did not yet simply label it a 'dark nest of bureaucrats',[17] as he did in later life, his diary entries, after a few years in his job, became critical. Brod records one of his remarks about the injured workmen: 'How modest these men are. They come to us and

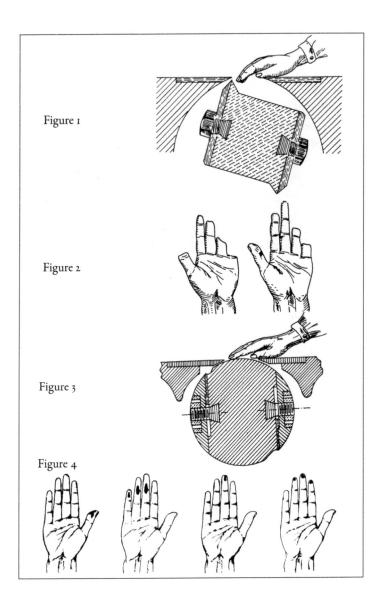

Figure 1

Figure 2

Figure 3

Figure 4

Skyscrapers in Gablonz.

beg. Instead of storming the institute and smashing it to little pieces, they come and beg.'[18]

During the first few years, Kafka undertook numerous official trips to the administrative districts that had been assigned to him, around *Reichenberg* (Liberec) in Northern Bohemia. This was then one of the most highly developed industrial regions in Europe, the industrial heartland of the monarchy, with huge textile mills, mechanical engineering plants and glass cutting and grinding works. Its fast-growing towns such as *Gablonz* (Jablonec nad Nisou) already boasted 'American skyscrapers'. By 1900, the factories in this region, mostly founded in the last decade of the 19th century, had vast 'sheds', in each of which several hundred workers stood below long transmission shafts to which they could attach their machines by belts. They worked in 12-hour shifts, day and night, which was why these sheds had electric light, long before the towns did.*

---

*Kafka's factories. The four administrative districts assigned to Kafka were in

One of Kafka's duties was to assign these enterprises to 'risk categories': he had to examine whether the actual danger to the workmen was in line with the information given to the Insurance Institute. Inevitably it was work that led to conflicts, but it gave him extensive insights into an inhuman industrial system, well beyond those of any other writer of his generation.

These experiences revived Kafka's social and political interests, first incited at the *Gymnasium* in discussions with Rudolf Illowý, and particularly intensified between 1908 and 1912, interests that distinguished him very clearly from the superficial opinions of most Prague Germans. Frequently – always alone – he would attend public meetings of the leading Czech politicians and follow day-to-day politics in *Čas* (*Time*), the paper published by T G Masaryk, later to become the first president of Czechoslovakia. Not even his friend Max Brod was aware that he frequently attended meetings

---

Northern Bohemia, the most important industrial centre of the Habsburg empire, with engineering, textile and glass enterprises – most of them exceedingly modern factories with up to 2,000 workers.

Kafka travelled through this region in order to check the 'classification' of these plants into risk categories and to recommend accident prevention measures. However, the Insurance Institute, with its 230 employees, was powerless to alter conditions in the factories. Not only did it have to administer more than 200,000 businesses, it also had to deal with a strong employers' lobby. In October 1911, a representative of the employers reminded the articled clerk Dr Kafka that 'thought and eyes at work' were 'the best protection against any accident'.

Average weekly hours were 66 – six working days of 11 hours – with an average hourly wage of 30 heller. At the time, this would buy a litre of milk or 900 grams of bread. A kilogram of margarine or a kilogram of beef cost 1 crown and 95 heller respectively, which meant that a worker would have to work six and a half hours to buy them.

One-off compensation in the event of disablement was likewise pitiful, at an average of 1,000 crowns, that is, a year's wages. These were truly 'workers without property'.

Textile factory in Northern Bohemia, in one of the
four administrative districts assigned to Kafka.

of the revolutionary socialist *Klub mladých*. At election meetings,
he listened to the speeches of the National Democrat, Dr Kramář,
of the Czech nationalist and socialist, Klofáč, and especially those
of the Social Democrat, Dr František Soukup. Soukup's assertion
that the 'dishonest ownership of the Germans would collapse' and
that 'national peace could only be the result of a compromise',[19] was
certainly close to Kafka's own attitude, and his lecture on the American electoral system on 1 June 1912 (on which Kafka made notes)
influenced the election scene in his novel *America* (originally called
Missing).

The most significant of these encounters was Kafka's participa-
tion in the workers' association 'Vilem Körber' and in the meetings of the *Klub mladých* (Young People's Club), an association of
different groups of young people for the dissemination of socialist

Auflöfung einer anarchiftifchen Jugend-organifation. Die Statthalterei hat die hiefige anarchiftifche Jugenborganifation „Klub mladých" (Klub ber Jungen) wegen Propagierung a n t i m i-l i t a r i ft i fcher und anberer ftaatsgefährlicher Jbeen aufgelöft.

On 10 October 1910, the 'anarchist youth organisation' *Klub mladých* was dissolved by the authorities, who accused it of 'anti-military propaganda and other ideas dangerous to the state'.

and anti-militarist ideas, which organised public lectures and dem-onstrations for various causes and anniversaries, such as the 40th anniversary of the Paris Commune. Kafka's well-attested participa-tion in these events has been sometimes exaggerated or inaccurately recorded, but political conditions at the time were not so free from risk that he could have safely recorded his opinions and experiences. In his notes on his reading we find the names, but nothing more, of radical political thinkers such as Bakunin, Belinsky, Herzen and Kropotkin. He also showed interest in the Chaluz movement in Pal-estine, which realised some of the ideas of the unsuccessful Russian revolution of 1905. In Max Brod's novel *The Magic Kingdom of Love*, written a few years after Kafka's death and whose character Garta represents his dead friend, Garta says: 'Perhaps one ought to join a workers' organisation.' [20] And in March 1918, towards the end of the First World War, Kafka himself drafted, as mentioned above, a plan for a *Brotherhood of Workers without Property*, divided into *Duties and Rights*.[21]

During the years preceding the First World War, Kafka made the acquaintance of the most important members of the as yet unknown Czech avant-garde – Frána Šrámek, S K Neumann, František Langer, Jaroslav Hašek, Michal Kácha, Artur Longen – and encountered the theoretical foundations of socialism. In addition, he regularly

Kafka c.1910/11.

attended the lectures and soirées of the lively Berta Fanta, wife of a Prague pharmacist, where many intellectuals met – the mathematician Kowalewski, the physicist Frank, the philosopher Ehrenfels and the young Albert Einstein (at that time teaching in Prague). There, Kafka heard talks on relativity, Planck's quantum theory and the principles of psychoanalysis. Shortly before writing his main works, Kafka was already familiar with all the most important problems and ideas of his age. He was, contrary to legend, far from being an ignorant country bumpkin.

Kafka's visits to the Fanta evenings may also have stimulated his renewed interest in religious problems. The religious diversity within that family – whose members included Muslims, atheists, Buddhists and theosophists – clearly reflected the uncertainty to which the emancipation of the Jews had led. (Kafka's brief interest

The Yiddish actor Yitzhak Löwy in the role of the 'wild man'.

in the Austrian educationalist and philosopher Rudolf Steiner was also aroused by Frau Fanta.) In Kafka, any thoughts of religion were clouded by his parents' example of ossified ritual faith; even as a child he had found religious ceremonies boring and ridiculous. Later, however, the questionable enlightenment and snobbish mysticism of those around him came to seem equally suspect, and, insofar as he had a religious development, it was in the direction of Judaism. Christianity scarcely played a role in it.

Kafka's opposition to the pseudo-religious derivatives he encountered also explains his attraction to the incomparably 'more lively' religion of the eastern European Jews, which he first experienced in 1910 and 1911 in the guest performances of a Yiddish theatrical group from Lviv in Ukraine (formerly Lemberg). Needless to say, the Prague-Jewish establishment ignored them, declaring that its actors were 'starvelings, tramps, fellow Jews',[22] the Yiddish plays mere barnstorming, and the venues questionable.

Kafka regularly attended the performances and made friends – very much to his father's chagrin – with one of the actors, Yitzhak Löwy. He organised for him an evening of readings from Yiddish literature (which Kafka himself introduced), corresponded with him over the next few years and as much as seven years later, in *Zürau* (now Sirem), edited Löwy's memoirs for a journal. Kafka's numerous accounts of performances and synopses of the plays account for well over a hundred pages in his diaries. At about the same time, he read a lengthy history of the Jews and a historical outline of Yiddish literature. His notes on his reading demonstrate a remarkably inadequate grounding in his own religion: thus, he did not even know the significance or the history of the Wailing Wall in Jerusalem.[23]

Kafka's efforts to explore his Jewishness, right into his final years, remained fragmentary. As he wrote to Brod in 1917, the Hasidic* stories are 'the only Jewish literature in which I immediately and always feel at home, quite apart from my own state of mind. With all the rest I am only wafted in'.[24] Around the same time, he began to learn Hebrew, though in 1929 he still writes of 'the absence of any firm Jewish ground under my feet'.[25] Not until six months before his death did he begin more intensive studies at the Berlin Academy for Jewish Studies.

His attitude to Zionism, the new point of orientation for many of his generation (for his friends Max Brod and Felix Weltsch and for his schoolmate Hugo Bergmann, who emigrated to Palestine shortly

---

*Hasidism was a movement for religious renewal which began among Jews of 18th-century eastern Europe. Its leaders communicated through fables and parables. Selections from these stories were published in German versions by the Jewish theologian and existentialist Martin Buber from 1906 onwards and attracted immense interest.

before the First World War) was equivocal. Its inflammatory and polemical style was strange to Kafka, as were the often rather academic and theoretical discussions about it that he had followed with great interest in 1912. But he did take note of the Zionists' colonising endeavours and the structure of the new settlements, and made repeated plans between 1912 and 1923 to travel to Palestine. He was particularly attracted by the solidarity and unselfishness in the volunteer communities and by the modest way of life of the new settlers. (There may be an element here of his attraction to his father's idea of an 'active life'. In 1913, Kafka worked in a plant nursery in the Prague district of Nusle and as late as 1917/18 advised his sister Ottla in her agricultural endeavours in *Zürau* [Sirem].)

About 1910, Kafka made his first major trips. In September 1909, he went to Riva on Lake Garda with Max Brod and his brother Otto; during an excursion to the Brescia Air Week he wrote 'Aeroplanes in Brescia' – one of his earliest published articles and the first description of these machines in German literature. In October 1910, he travelled to Paris, again with Max and Otto Brod, then in August 1911 to northern Italy, Paris and Lucerne with Max Brod, though he stayed on for a week at the sanatorium Erlenbach near Zurich on his own. In 1912, he went to Weimar with Max Brod but spent three weeks at the Jungborn Nature Treatment Sanatorium in the Harz Mountains afterwards.

These trips were attempts to loosen up his Prague isolation. 'How do I live in Prague, after all?' he wrote in 1912. 'This craving for people, which I have and which is transformed into anxiety once it is fulfilled, finds an outlet only during vacations.'[26] And in the last year of his life he wrote to Brod: 'At the time we had truly innocent innocence – perhaps that's not worth regretting – and the evil powers, whether on good or bad assignments, were only lightly fingering the entrances through which they were going to penetrate someday, an event to which they were already looking forward with unbearable

Battery, Lower End of Manhattan Island, New York.

In 1905, Alfred Löwy, Kafka's uncle, sent this postcard
to his parents. Kafka himself never saw America.

rejoicing.'[27] Their last joint trip was in 1912. In the autumn of that
year, came the crucial turning point: until then the basic form of
his life was not yet finally fixed. As Kafka later noted in his diary:
'Always this one principal anguish: If I had gone away in 1912, in full
possession of all my forces, with a clear head, not eaten by the strain
of keeping down living forces!'[28]

6

The Only Way to Write!

B Y 1912, KAFKA'S GRADUAL PROCESS of withdrawal and isolation was almost complete and virtually beyond the reach of any outside influence. In an article about the periodical *Hyperion*, which had ceased publication but which had published some of his earliest works (in 1908, 'The Trees', 'Clothes', 'Rejection', 'The Tradesman', 'Absent-minded Window-gazing', 'The Way Home', 'Passers-by', 'On the Tram'; in 1909, the two conversations from 'Description of a Struggle'), Kafka wrote: 'Those whom their nature keeps away from the community ... need no defence because incomprehension cannot affect them because they are dark, and they find love everywhere. Nor do they need any sustenance, for, if they want to remain truthful, they can draw only on their own substance, so that one cannot help them without first doing them harm.'[1]

In the autumn of that year, a determined concentration of his strength resulted in Kafka's first major works – the best part (chapters one to seven) of the novel *Der Veßchollere* (*Amerika*) and the two stories *The Judgement* and *The Metamorphosis*. The first to be written down, in the night of 22/23 September, was *The Judgement*. Immediately afterwards, Kafka noted in his diary: 'The fearful strain

The Čech-Bridge across the Vltava River in Prague.
In the top-floor flat of the building on the left Kafka
wrote *The Judgement* and *The Metamorphosis*.

and joy, how the story developed before me, as if I were advancing
over water. Several times during this night I heaved my own weight
on my back. How everything can be said, how for everything, for
the strangest fancies, there waits a great fire in which they perish and
rise up again ... The conviction verified that with my novel-writing I
am in the shameful lowlands of writing. This is the only way to write,
only with such coherence, with such a complete opening out of the
body and the soul.'[2]

The remark about 'the shameful lowlands of writing' refers to
the first version of *Amerika*; a few days later, Kafka started a new
version. Within a few weeks he wrote more than six chapters but
was interrupted in the seventh chapter, between mid-November
and early December, by *The Metamorphosis*. After this, he continued
with *Amerika* only slowly and abandoned it a month later, until the

autumn of 1914.* His two later attempts at a full-length narrative, *The Trial* and *The Castle*, also remained fragments. Only in *context*, at night and in complete isolation, was Kafka able to work. Inevitably, his productivity fluctuated greatly. Between February 1913 and July 1914 not a single major work was written. But then, between 22 September and 6 December – just 74 days – he produced over 400 manuscript pages. During the same time he wrote over 60 letters to his fiancée, often of more than ten pages. *The Judgement*, written in eight hours, runs to 20 manuscript pages.

Kafka himself always regarded 1912 as a crucial turning point. A decade later he wrote to Milena Jesenská about *The Judgement*: 'Each sentence in that story, each word, each – if I may say so – music is connected with "fear". On this occasion the wound broke open for the first time during one long night.'[3] It is significant that time and again, Kafka speaks of spectres, of the 'fear' which had then appeared for the first time, and of the 'innocent innocence' of the time before, of a 'no-man's-land, a floating, a nothing'.[4] At the

---

*Missing/Amerika. The fragmentary novel which Kafka called *The Man who Went Missing*, and which Max Brod published after his death under the title *Amerika*, begins with a boy sailing to America in search of a new life. But *Amerika* seems to replicate the injustice, abuse and violence of Europe: 'As Karl Rossmann, a poor boy of 16 who had been packed off to America by his parents because a servant girl had seduced him and got herself with child by him, stood on the liner slowly entering the harbour of New York, a sudden burst of sunshine seemed to illumine the Statue of Liberty, so that he saw it in a new light, although he had sighted it long before. The arm with the sword rose up as if newly stretched aloft.' Rather than the real America of 1911, which Kafka knew from travel books and from relatives who had emigrated there, this is an ultra-modern, ruthlessly efficient dystopia where the rich live in town apartments and country estates while the poor inhabit slums or roam the country roads, and those in between are obliged to work incessantly as the servants of machines. After many serio-comic adventures, Karl's quest for justice takes him to the enigmatic Theatre of Oklahoma, which offers 'employment for everyone, a place for everyone'.

moment when he becomes aware of this state, fear is born. (Kierkeg-aard writes: 'That is the deepest secret of innocence: namely that it is also fear. In a dream, the intellect projects its own reality, but this reality turns out to be nothingness'.)

From then on this word, 'fear', appears time and again in his diaries and in his letters: fear of the outside world bursting into his own reality; fear of destroying even this inner freedom by guilt; remorse over a *life unlived*; fear of nothingness. In *The Concept of Dread*, Kierkegaard says:

> Though dread is afraid, yet it maintains a sly intercourse with its object, cannot look away from it, indeed will not, for if the individual wills this, then repentance sets in. If to one or another this may appear a difficult saying, I can do nothing about it. He who has the requisite firmness to be, if I may use the expression, a prosecuting attorney for the Deity, though not with respect to others, yet with respect to himself, will not find this saying difficult. Life, moreover, presents phenomena enough in which the individual in dread gazes almost desirously at guilt and yet fears it ... However, in view of all such cases, we have yet to wait until there come forward individuals who, in spite of their outward gifts, do not choose the broad way, but rather pain and distress and dread ... so that they lose as it were what it is only too seductive and dangerous to possess. Such a battle is indubitably very exhausting, since there will come moments when they almost regret having started upon this path, and sadly, yes, sometimes almost despairingly, they will think of the smiling path which would have stretched before them.[5]

A more accurate description of Kafka's situation is hardly pos-sible, and Kafka recognised it. In a diary entry of August 1913, after his first reading of Kierkegaard (he did not tackle the philosophical

Oskar Baum. Drawing
by Friedrich Feigl.

works until several years later), Kafka wrote: 'As I suspected, his case, despite essential differences, is very similar to mine, at least he is on the same side of the world. He bears me out like a friend.'[6] As late as 1922, he wrote to Max Brod: 'Why then this sense of repining, this repining that never ceases? Why always the conclusion: I could live and I do not live?'[7] This sense of guilt about a *life unlived* grew ever stronger during the final decade of Kafka's life, and with it his fear that his life was a *nothing, justified solely by his writing.**

---

*Danish philosopher and theologian Søren Kierkegaard (1813–55) is regarded as the intellectual forerunner of existentialism. In works such as *Fear and Trembling* and *Either/Or* (both 1843), Kierkegaard emphasised the importance of individual choice based not on abstract principles or rationality, but on a 'leap of faith'. Kafka was fascinated by Kierkegaard's acute psychological analysis

A clear distinction must be drawn here between Kafka's *yearning* for a 'normal' life and his *determination* never to give in to such a yearning. It is wrong to regard Kafka as a saint prevented only by hostile circumstances from being a loving family man and a sociable person. It is true that he longed for a normal life, but he was also determined never to yield to that longing. All his attempts – and there were enough of them – to yield to normality foundered not on the persons or circumstances involved, but on himself, who regarded such matters as a betrayal of a life dedicated to literature. Some of his attempts to satisfy the outside world were only meant – as in the dreams of the schoolboy – to avoid attracting *public attention* to himself. The most shocking example of this – and one of Kafka's most important observations on the situation of the writer – is his refusal of an invitation from his friend Oskar Baum to spend his holidays with him. He wrote about it to Max Brod in July 1922:

It is a fear of change, a fear of attracting the attention of the gods by what is a major act for a person of my sort.

Last night, as I lay sleepless and let everything veer back and forth between my aching temples, what I had almost forgotten ... became clear to me: namely, on what frail ground or rather altogether non-existent ground I live, over a darkness from which the dark power emerges when it wills and heedless of my stammering, destroys my life. Writing sustains me, but is it not more accurate to say that it sustains this kind of life? But I don't

---

of the 'dread' (Angst) that preceded this, although he often remained unwilling to make this existential leap. In the 20th century, Kierkegaard's assertion of the self-defining freedom of the individual proved highly influential with philosophers such as Jean-Paul Sartre and Martin Heidegger, as well as writers such as Max Frisch and Samuel Beckett. Like Kafka, Kierkegaard became engaged to be married only to break it off after a year of soul-searching, deciding that he could not combine his writing with married life.

mean, of course, that my life is better when I don't write. Rather it is much worse then and wholly unbearable and has to end in madness. But that, granted, only follows from the postulate that I am a writer, which is actually true even when I am not writing, and a non-writing writer is a monster inviting madness.

But what about being a writer itself? Writing is a sweet and wonderful reward, but for what? In the night it became clear to me, as clear as in an object lesson to a child, that it is the reward for serving the devil. This descent to the dark powers, this unshackling of spirits bound by nature, these dubious embraces and whatever else may take place in the nether parts which the higher parts no longer know, when one writes one's stories in the sunshine. Perhaps there are other forms of writing, but I know only this kind; at night, when fear keeps me from sleeping, I know only this kind.

And the diabolic element in it seems very clear to me. It is vanity and sensuality which continually buzz about one's own or even another's form – and feast on him. The movement multiplies itself – it is a regular solar system of vanity. Sometimes a naïve person will wish, 'I would like to be dead and see how everyone mourns me.' Such a writer is continually staging such a scene: He dies (or rather he does not live) and continually mourns himself. From this springs a terrible fear of death, which need not reveal itself as fear of death but may also appear as fear of change …

The reasons for this fear of death may be divided into two main categories. First, he has a terrible fear of dying because he has not yet lived. By this I do not mean that wife and child, fields and cattle are essential to living. What is essential to life is only to forgo complacency, to move into the house instead of admiring it and hanging garlands around it. In reply to this one might say that this is a matter of fate and is not given into anyone's hand. But then why this sense of repining, this repining that never ceases? To make oneself finer and more savoury? That is a part of it. But why do such nights leave one always with the conclusion: I could live and I do not live?

The second reason – perhaps it is all really one, the two do not want to stay apart for me now – is the belief 'What I have play-acted is really going to happen. I have not bought myself off by my writing ...'

To underscore the whole story in terms of my writing – but I do not do the underscoring, the thing underscores itself – I must add that my fear of the journey is partly compounded by the thought that I will be kept away from the desk for at least several days. And this ridiculous thought is really the only legitimate one, since the existence of the writer is truly dependent upon his desk and if he wants to keep madness at bay he must never go far from his desk, he must hold on to it with his teeth ...

I have sent Oskar a telegram, cancelling. There was no help for it. It was the only way I could deal with my agitation. Yesterday's first letter to him struck a familiar note for me. That is how I used to write to F. [8]

F. is Felice Bauer, his future fiancée, whom Kafka met at Max Brod's on 13 August 1912. Towards the end of October, a correspondence began between them, continuing for several years, until 1917 – over 500 letters and postcards. However, within a few weeks, in December, when Kafka declined a Christmas visit to Berlin, where Bauer lived, and shortly afterwards gave up work on *Der Verschellere* (*Amerika*), he confirmed the truth of his remark (made ten years later) 'that it was certain that, should I have ever been happy, outside of writing and whatever is connected with it (I don't rightly know if I ever was) – at such times I was incapable of writing, with the result that everything had barely begun when the whole applecart tipped over, for the longing to write was always uppermost'.[9]

For these reasons, after 1912, Kafka no longer entered into any friendships (with the exception of the more fatherly relationship with the young medical student Robert Klopstock during the final three years of his life); for these reasons he remained in Prague; for these reasons he dissolved his three engagements (1914, 1916, 1919), as well as his relationships with the *Swiss girl* [Gerti Wasner] (1913), Grete Bloch (after 1914) and Milena Jesenská (after 1920). Only his last relationship, with Dora Diamant, six months before his death, was lit up by a certain euphoria.

These *attempts to get married* and his friendships with women were, of course, under an additional strain – society's questionable ideas of sex, marriage and morality prior to the First World War, ideas shared by Kafka's father and accurately described by Karl Kraus: 'The founders of the norms reversed the relations between the sexes: the female sex is corseted in convention and the male sex is unleashed.' [10] The same sexual etiquette that subjected middle-class daughters to the ideal of virginity demanded that middle-class sons gained knowledge and experience that they could acquire only in the brothel. Therefore, in Prague, along with cabarets and nightclubs, there were a large number of brothels, some of which enjoyed a high reputation among roués and the literati. Franz Werfel dedicated his story 'The House of Mourning' to one of the most famous of them, in *Gamsgasse* (Kamzíková), only a few steps from the Kinsky Palace:

> The Grand Salon was absolutely first class: Renaissance furniture, heavily gilt; red velvet curtains and a parquetry dance floor smooth as glass. This was, in short, an establishment which could tranquilly repudiate the name applied to it by a poverty-stricken and inarticulate vocabulary ... For everything here mirrored for the beholder – if rather self-consciously

in such a setting – the period of the Dual Monarchy: the plush furniture, the gilded arabesques, the etchings, ... the dust-traps, the moth-eaten sumptuousness, even the Imperial portrait hanging in the kitchen – all these were a survival of the Renaissance splendours of a proud and vanished decade ...

The ladies, except those on private service, were all at their posts. They paced the room with swaying step, made rapturous eyes at themselves in the mirrors, coolly helped themselves to the guests' cigarettes, and now and then with detached and condescending air sat for a while at the tables. They seemed to be full of a consciousness of their own dignity, a dignity which communicated itself to every *pensionnaire* of this famous and superior establishment. To be received here was to have entry to the upper circles.[11]

There is no doubt that Kafka, during the years after gaining his law degree, also subjected himself to this prescribed sexual snobbery, even though the forms of this peculiar *gourmandise* always remained alien to him, if only because of his anxiety. His encounters with prostitutes scarcely exhibited the pretended indifference of his contemporaries. Instead, they too reflected a secret longing for fellowship, albeit in the same vein as his search, in his early story 'The Street Window', for 'any arm at all' to which 'one might cling'. In 1908, Kafka wrote to Brod: 'I am so urgently driven to find someone who will merely touch me in a friendly manner that yesterday I went to the hotel with a prostitute. She is too old to still be melancholic, but feels sorry, though it doesn't surprise her, that people are not as kind to prostitutes as they are to a mistress. I didn't comfort her since she didn't comfort me either.'[12]

Kafka later regarded his few relationships with such women as *unclean*. It is all the more interesting that in his great novels, the prostitute is virtually the *only* kind of woman we encounter: first in

Amerika in the person of Brunelda, a bloated flesh colossus of exclusively passive sexuality, and even more so in his two later novels, *The Trial* and *The Castle*, in the persons of Fräulein Bürstner or the servant girls Leni and Frieda, washerwomen and kept mistresses of lawyers, castellans and officials. They are dulled carnal creatures thinking only of 'present slight physical defects' and emitting 'a bitter, exciting odour as of pepper'.[13]

Degraded women, whores by profession or opportunity, recur in these novels, albeit with a very precise function in the plot. At culminating moments, in situations that are decisive for the main character's future fate, they draw him – often in the literal sense – down to themselves and obstruct him, invariably deluding him that this would serve his *case* best. Thus, in *The Trial*: "'I seem to recruit women helpers," he [the bank official K] thought almost in surprise. "First Fräulein Bürstner, then the wife of the Law Court Attendant, and now this little nurse who appears to have some incomprehensible passion for me."'[14]

Yet by getting involved with 'this little nurse', Leni, Josef K misses an important conversation with his lawyer and the office director. Similarly, K, the land surveyor in *The Castle*, crosses the very official who has to deal with his application, Klamm, by taking his mistress Frieda from him. Here, more clearly than anywhere else in his novels, Kafka describes 'his' situation – at the very point in the manuscript where he changes from the first person singular used until then to the neutral 'K'.

They embraced each other, her little body burned in K's hands, in a state of unconsciousness which K tried again and again but in vain to master as they rolled a little way, landing with a thud on Klamm's door, where they lay among the small puddles of beer and other refuse gathered on the floor, There, hours went past, hours in which they breathed as one, in which their hearts beat as one, hours in which K was haunted by the feeling that he was losing himself or wandering into a strange country, farther than man had ever wandered before, a country so strange that not even the air had anything in common with his native air, where one might die of strangeness, and yet whose enchantment was such that one could only go on and lose oneself further.[15]

Kafka's female characters are, in a sense, conceived as whores. Fusion with them is such that it cannot lead to marriage, that it can take place only in a state of 'unconsciousness'. 'Temptations' occur only in a 'strange country', fulfilling Kafka's innermost wish – to yield to his longing for fellowship in a setting that excluded the possibility of fellowship. That fellowship (Kafka was convinced) would have meant the end of his writing and, therefore, could exist only as an ideal whose attainment would have required other preconditions. These women are the true epitome of the moving and suicidal struggle for 'purity' that filled the final decade of his life.

The pattern of this struggle had been laid down early. In 1907, Kafka wrote to a woman friend – and one can already almost hear the tone of his later letters to women: '... If you are a little fond of me, it's out of pity; my part is fear.'[16] These were the conditions under which his *marriage attempts* began: 'I grew up more or less like a businessman who lives from day to day, with worries and forebodings, but without keeping proper accounts.'[17]

A few days after his first encounter with his future fiancée, Kafka noted in his diary:

Fräulein Felice Bauer. When I arrived at Brod's on 13 August, she was sitting at the table and really did remind me of a servant girl. I was not at all curious about who she was, but rather took her for granted at once. Bony, empty face that wore its emptiness openly. Bare throat. A blouse thrown on. Looked very domestic in her dress although, as it later turned out, she by no means was. (I alienate myself from her a little by inspecting her so closely. What a state I'm in now, indeed, alienated in general from the whole of everything good, and don't even believe it yet ...) Almost broken nose. Blonde, somewhat straight, unattractive hair, strong chin. As I was taking my seat I looked at her closely for the first time, by the time I was seated I already had an unshakeable opinion.[18]

Four weeks later, on 20 September (two days before writing down *The Judgement*), Kafka wrote the first letter to Berlin, where Bauer worked in the office of a Parlograph (an early type of Dictaphone) firm. As a pretext, he used a trip to Palestine that had been loosely agreed between them. Evidently she replied only briefly and then remained silent for the next three weeks to Kafka's letters, who was meanwhile trying, with the help of friends, to get her to reply. About the same time, on 8 October, he wrote the long letter to Max Brod, in which, in the middle of his work on *Amerika*, he complained that his parents were insisting that on his free afternoons over the next two weeks he should supervise the Prague Asbestos Factory Hermann & Co, which belonged to his brother-in-law and in which Kafka's father had bought him a share:

I stood for a long time at the window and pressed against the pane, and there were many moments when it would have suited me to alarm the toll collector on the bridge by my fall. But all the while I really felt too firm to let the decision to smash myself to pieces on the pavement penetrate to the proper decisive depth. It also seemed to me that my staying alive interrupts my writing less than death – even if I can speak only, only of interruption and that between the beginning of the novel and its continuation in two weeks somehow, in the factory especially and especially in relationship to my satisfied parents, I shall move and have my being within the innermost spaces of my novel ...

And yet, now in the morning, I must not conceal this, I hate them all, one after the other, and think that in these 14 days I shall scarcely be able to summon up the good-mornings and good-evenings. But hatred – and this is again directed against myself – really belongs more outside the window than peacefully sleeping in bed. I am far less sure than I was during the night.[19]

By pleading with Kafka's mother, Max Brod was able to avert this disaster, just as, a few weeks later, when Bauer was worried about Kafka's behaviour, he urged her in two letters to make some allowance 'for Franz and his often morbid sensibility' and to 'help him over his conflicts by understanding and kindness, remembering that such a unique and wonderful person is entitled to be treated somewhat differently'.[20]

Kafka's *hatred* and 'sensitivity' were caused mainly by the timetable, which he followed for the first time during those months of productivity since mid-September. All his future periods of creativity used the same schedule, which he jokingly called his 'military exercise life'.[21] After his office hours (from eight in the morning to two in the afternoon) he would go home, sleep from about three to half past seven, go for an hour's walk, either with friends or alone, have dinner with his family (eating late was customary among the Prague middle classes) and then begin to write at about 11 at night, working until two or three in the morning, sometimes even later.

On 23 October, Kafka finally received the long-awaited reply from Felice Bauer, and from that moment on their correspondence – with two, three or four letters a day – assumed an almost boundless character. Kafka wrote to her about his family, his plans,

---

Grosser Lärm

Ich sitze in meinem Zimmer im Hauptquartier des Lärms der ganzen Wohnung. Alle Türen höre ich schlagen, durch ihren Lärm bleiben mir nur die Schritte der zwischen ihnen Laufenden erspart, noch das Zuklappen der Herdtüre in der Küche höre ich. Der Vater durchbricht die Türen meines Zimmers und zieht im nachschleppenden Schlafrock durch, aus dem Ofen im Nebenzimmer wird die Asche gekratzt, Valli fragt, durch das Vorzimmer Wort für Wort rufend, ob des Vaters Hut schon geputzt ist, ein Zischen, das mir befreundet sein will, erhebt noch das Geschrei einer antwortenden Stimme. Die Wohnungstüre wird aufgeklinkt und lärmt, wie aus katarrhalischem Hals, öffnet sich dann weiterhin mit dem Singen einer Frauenstimme und schliesst sich endlich mit einem dumpfen, männlichen Ruck, der sich am rücksichtslosesten anhört. Der Vater ist weg, jetzt beginnt der zartere, zerstreutere, hoffnungslosere Lärm, von den Stimmen der zwei Kanarienvögel angeführt. Schon früher dachte ich daran, bei den Kanarienvögeln fällt es mir von neuem ein, ob ich nicht die Türe bis zu einer kleinen Spalte öffnen, schlangengleich ins Nebenzimmer kriechen und so auf dem Boden meine Schwestern und ihr Fräulein um Ruhe bitten sollte. *Franz Kafka*

44

---

the progress of his work on *The Man Who Went Missing* (*Amerika*) and *The Metamorphosis*. He also described to her his daily schedule. When she asked why he had chosen such a timetable, he sent her his sketch 'Great Noise' which had recently been published in a short-lived Prague literary periodical, *Herder-Blätter*, edited by Willy Haas. (Kafka had taken this piece of prose from his diary, making only a few changes.)

> I am sitting in my room in the headquarters of all the noise in
> the whole flat. I hear all the doors banging, and this noise only
> spares me the footsteps of those walking between them. I even
> hear the shutting of the oven door in the kitchen. Father bursts
> through the doors of my room and walks across it, his dressing
> gown trailing behind him. Somebody is scraping the ash from
> the stove next door. Valli asks, shouting each word across the
> front room, whether father's hat has been cleaned already
> and a hiss, which is well intentioned towards me, heightens
> the screaming answer. The front door handle is pushed down

Kafka's letter to his first publisher, Ernst Rowohlt.

with a noise like that coming from a catarrh-infected throat, then the door opens wide, sounding like a female voice, and finally shuts again with a dull, male thump, which sounds the most inconsiderate of all. Father is gone and the gentler, more absent-minded and hopeless noise starts, introduced by the voices of the two canaries. I had thought it before; now the two canaries make me think again, whether it would not be a good idea to open the door a tiny bit, slither into the neighbouring room like a snake and from the floor beg my sisters and their nanny to be quiet.[22]

Willy Haas and the Prague Herder Association also invited Kafka to give his first public reading – on only one other occasion did he read publicly from his own work. The reading was on 4 December: he read *The Judgement*, which, dedicated to Felice Bauer, appeared a few months later in Max Brod's annual almanac *Arkadia*. That

December also saw the publication of Kafka's first book, a collection of 18 short prose pieces under the title *Meditation*, which Kafka, with Brod's help, had submitted to the German publishing house Rowohlt. Kurt Wolff, who joined Rowohlt as a partner shortly after its founding by Ernst Rowohlt in 1908, took over the publishing house completely in the autumn of 1912, and in 1913 renamed it Kurt Wolff Verlag. Wolff went on to publish all of Kafka's subsequent books. The first, in May 1913, was *The Stoker* (the first chapter of what would eventually be published as *Amerika*), which appeared as Volume 3 of the *Day of Judgement* series.*

Kafka got on well with 'this courteous publisher ... a very handsome man of about 25, whom God has endowed ... with a taste for publishing and a little publisher's sense'. Wolff invariably met the often demanding wishes of his author, even though, as Kafka wrote to a friend in 1918, he was 'a publisher who is besieged by authors'[23] and even though Kafka's writings often appeared in print runs of just 800 or 1,000 copies. Only *The Stoker*, *The Metamorphosis* and *The Judgement* (all published in the very affordable *Day of Judgement* series) sold well enough to be reprinted.†

---

*'From Kafka's story [The Stoker] there emerges a primal drive towards goodness, no resentment but something of a childhood's buried passion for the good; that emotion of excited children's prayers and something of the restless application of meticulous schoolwork, and much for which one cannot coin an expression other than moral gentleness. The demands of what one should do are raised here by a conscience that is not driven by ethical principles, but by a delicate urgent sensibility, which is continually discovering small matters of great significance and which reveals strange layers in questions that for others are just a smooth block of indifference.' ROBERT MUSIL

†Only seven books were published or accepted for publication during Kafka's lifetime:

Meditation (*Betrachtung*), 100 pages in a large type (Tertia), numbered edition of 800 copies (Rowohlt, Leipzig, 1912).

The Stoker: A Fragment (*Der Heizer: Ein Fragment*), 48 pages, print run of

In one of his first letters to Felice, Kafka wrote that his thinking about her was connected to his writing. During the weeks that followed, and with growing intimacy, his statements became more definite, the more so as he regarded Felice – like his friend Max Brod – as a secure, strong, calm and 'businesslike' person. (When she once hinted at something contrary, he answered, downright outraged, that she obviously wanted to disguise herself and frighten him.)

By the beginning of December, Kafka was already preparing Felice for his decision not to come to Berlin during the Christmas holidays (this would have been their first opportunity to see each other again); by then, he was working on the conclusion of *The Metamorphosis* and was afraid of any external irritation (which a journey, even a short one, always was for him). Henceforth, even the tenderest declaration of love was not without a hint of how difficult its realisation would be. A week earlier, he had quoted in a letter to Bauer a poem by the 18th-century Chinese poet Yuan Tzu-tsai, a poem he had loved for many years, since Hans Heilmann's prose translations of Chinese poetry had inspired some passages in his early story 'Description of a Struggle': [24]

---

about 1,000. Volume 3 of the series *Day of Judgement* (*Der jüngste Tag*) (Wolff, Leipzig, 1913).

The Metamorphosis (*Die Verwandlung*), 80 pages, print run of about 1,000, Volume 22/23 of the series *Day of Judgement* (*Der jüngste Tag*) (Wolff, Leipzig, 1915).

The Judgement (*Das Urteil*), 32 pages, print run of about 1,000, Volume 34 of the series *Day of Judgement* (*Der jüngste Tag*) (Wolff, Leipzig, 1916).

In the Penal Colony (*In der Strafkolonie*), 72 pages, bibliophile print of the W Drugulin printing works, print run of 1,000 (Wolff, Leipzig, 1919).

A Country Doctor (*Ein Landarzt*), short stories, 192 pages in a large type (Tertia), print run of about 1,000 (Wolff, Leipzig, 1919 [published 1920]).

A Hunger Artist (*Ein Hungerkünstler*), stories, 88 pages, print run of about 2,000 (Die Schmiede, Berlin, 1924 [published posthumously]).

Kurt Wolff, who became Kafka's publisher. Portrait by Felice Casorati, 1925.

In the Dead of Night
In the cold night, while poring over
my book, I forgot the hour of bedtime.
The scent of my gold-embroidered bedcover
has already evaporated, the fireplace burns no more.
My beautiful mistress, who hitherto has controlled
her wrath with difficulty, snatches away the lamp,
And asks: Do you know how late it is?

In his correspondence, Kafka keeps returning to this poem, interpreting it as a fundamental situation – whose relevance to his 'military exercise life' was clear enough anyway – and subsequently asking an (even sharper) question: what if the woman in the poem was not the man's mistress but his wife and that night had only been one typical night of all the nights of that marriage?

So, 1912 ended with a bleak outlook for Felice Bauer, who had reciprocated Kafka's love but not seen him again in person even once. As he came closer to loving her, Kafka felt his creativity was leaving him – and he hinted as much to her. Having interrupted his writing of *Amerika* to write *The Metamorphosis*, he found it hard to resume. He only managed to produce a few more pages and then in January gave up work on it. Another prose attempt, the story of the character Ernst Liman, proved similarly unsuccessful. At any rate, the idea for *Amerika* now lay over a year back in Kafka's past. The experiences of a 16-year-old emigrant in a strange world had become in *The Judgement* the small world of a businessman who writes a letter to a friend of his youth who has moved abroad, telling him of his engagement. It is typical that, when he started this story during that night in September 1912, Kafka thought of describing a war and that it was only while he was writing that he dropped this external image of an inner condition.*

---

*Kafka knew America mainly from family reports. In 1905, his Uncle Alfred went to Washington for the 'Seventh Railroad Convention'; in 1911, his cousin Otto established an export business in New York; at about the same time, his 16-year-old brother Franz came to America to attend a boarding school near New York; his cousin Emil worked at the huge mail-order firm of Sears Roebuck in Chicago. Thus, Kafka, as he wrote to his publisher, had the 'most modern' America in mind when he wrote *Missing* (later published by Brod as *Amerika*). For instance, its enormous traffic – at a time when there were only a few hundred motorcars in the whole of Bohemia: 'The cars ... were actually touching each other, nosing each other forward. A pedestrian here and there, in a particular hurry to cross the road, would climb through the individual cars as if they were a public passage, not caring at all whether there was only a chauffeur in it and a couple of servants, or the most fashionable company. But that kind of behaviour seemed rather high-handed to Karl.'

This inner condition emerges even more clearly in *The Metamorphosis*. In *The Judgement*, the father still represents the world – the use of this motif places Kafka as still firmly within the literary tropes of his contemporaries, the early expressionist generation. But in *The Metamorphosis*, Gregor Samsa does literally what Raban (the lead character of 'Wedding Preparations in the Country') only dreams of: escaping the demands of the world by sending one's clothed body out into it while remaining in bed oneself and becoming a gigantic insect. The story is a self-portrait and a self-punishment in which Kafka finds a metaphorical form for his *phobia* of and sensitivity towards the outside world, manifested all too clearly in his sensitivity to noise, which became such an ordeal for his friends and neighbours in the final years of his life. Yet, at the same time, he is able to reflect consciously and ironically on his fears: he was fully aware of the 'last earthly remnants of the play-actor'[25] in himself. Even where Kafka gives a ruthlessly perceptive description of his 'life plan', he poses at its end a countervailing question – which we might also see as an alternative form of hope.

7

Life or Literature? Kafka's Engagements and *The Trial*

T̲HE DIARY ENTRIES for 1913 are in the seventh quarto note-book, at the end of which Kafka wrote: 'The notebook begins with F [Felice Bauer] who, on 2 May 1913, made me feel uncertain; this same beginning can serve as conclusion, too.'[1] Throughout 1913 and in the first half of 1914, Kafka wrote no major prose. In the spring of 1913, as he would often do again, he tried to overcome his 'self-torture' through activity – long walks, helping in a carpenter's shop, riding, swimming and rowing. (He was very fond of rowing and owned a boat on the *Moldau* [Vltava].) In April, he began to work in a plant nursery in Nusle in the afternoons. **Outwardly** at least, being also exceptionally handsome, tall and slim, he never had the quirks necessary to be some sort of ascetic stylite.

Over the Easter holidays, Kafka visited Felice Bauer in Berlin for the first time; on his second visit, at Whitsun, he was introduced to her family. Over the next few weeks, Kafka considered approaching her father, Carl Bauer, with a request for a formal engagement. But in the months that followed, his diary entries became more sceptical: 'The wish for an unthinking reckless solitude. To be face to face only with myself.'[2] In July, he set out – as he would several more times – 'a summary of all the arguments for and against my marriage';[3] on 15

August he decided: 'I'll shut myself off from everyone to the point of insensibility. Make an enemy of everyone, speak to no one.'[4] But that same day Kafka sent off a letter, no longer extant, to Carl Bauer. He was so impatient for an answer that six days later he drafted another letter in his diary:

> You hesitate to answer my request, that is quite understandable, any father would do the same in the case of any suitor. Hence, your hesitation is not the reason for this letter, at most it increases my hope for a calm and correct judgement of it. I am writing this letter because I fear that your hesitation or your considerations are caused by more general reflections, rather than by that single passage in my first letter which indeed makes them necessary and which might have given me away. That is the passage concerning the unbearableness of my job.
>
> You will perhaps pass over what I say, but you shouldn't, you should rather inquire into it very carefully, in which case I should carefully and briefly have to answer you as follows. My job is unbearable to me because it conflicts with my only desire and my only calling, which is literature. Since I am nothing but literature and can and want to be nothing else, my job will never take possession of me, it may, however, shatter me completely, and this is by no means a remote possibility. Nervous states of the worst sort control me without pause, and this year of worry and torment about my and your daughter's future has revealed to the full my inability to resist. You might ask why I do not give up this job and – I have no money – do not try to support myself by literary work. To this I can make only the miserable reply that I don't have the strength for it, and that, as far as I can see, I shall instead be destroyed by this job, and destroyed quickly.
>
> And now compare me to your daughter, this healthy, gay,

natural, strong girl. As often as I have repeated it to her in perhaps 500 letters [Kafka exaggerates a little] and as often as she has calmed me with a 'no' that to be sure has no very convincing basis, it nevertheless remains true that she must be unhappy with me, so far as I can see. I am, not only because of my external circumstances but even much more because of my essential nature, a reserved, silent, unsocial, dissatisfied person, but without being able to call this my misfortune, for it is only the reflection of my goal. Conclusions can at last be drawn from the sort of life I lead at home. Well, I live with my family, among the best and most loveable people, more strange than a stranger. I have not spoken an average of 20 words a day to my mother these last years, hardly ever said more than hello to my father. I do not speak at all to my married sisters and my brothers-in-law [Elli and Karl Hermann, Valli and Josef Pollak], and not because I have anything against them. The reason for it is simply this, that I have not the slightest thing to talk to them about. Everything that is not literature bores me and I hate it, for it disturbs me or delays me, if only because I think it does. I lack all aptitude for family life except, at best, as an observer. I have no family feeling and visitors make me almost feel as though I were maliciously being attacked.

A marriage could not change me, just as my job cannot change me.[5]

Carl Bauer would hardly have been delighted with this letter. Here is his future son-in-law informing him that his daughter is bound to be unhappy with him, that he will perish in his job, that literature is his only interest and that even marriage could not change that. Like 'Letter to his Father', this missive illustrates well Kafka's way of presenting relatively unambiguous circumstances, if he thought it threatened his writing, in an extremely ambiguous light, always attributing the fault to himself, that the final effect was always in his favour. He was undoubtedly aware of what he was doing – and that only sharpened the sting. Of course, he realised that the description of his *life at home* was exaggerated and in detail untrue. His diary proves that he spoke quite often with his parents and sisters – especially with Ottla, whom, significantly, he does not mention at all in the letter.

In any case, the answer from Carl Bauer arrived and Kafka never sent off his second letter. The answer contained consent, but Kafka never replied to it directly. Instead he wrote a letter to Felice Bauer, who probably did not pass it on to her father, since she asked Kafka for another version. He, however, declared himself unable to do so, invoking Grillparzer, Dostoevsky, Kleist and Flaubert[6] – authors he admired all his life.

Kafka frequently referred to the life patterns of these authors when he needed an interpretation or justification of his own actions. Again, their example allowed him to flinch from the decision, just as he had earlier allowed the plan for a joint holiday with Bauer to go awry. This first break with Bauer, in September 1913, sets the pattern for many very similar decisions in Kafka's later life: faced with a choice between 'life' and literature – whether genuine or not – he invariably decides in favour of literature, without wishing to decide against life. Inevitably, this conflict kept recurring. He 'escaped' from this first decision-making by travelling to Vienna to an International Congress on Lifesaving, which he attended with his director and his immediate superior. From Vienna he wrote to Felice Bauer several times, sending her some notes about the Zionist Congress which was being held there, and telling her about visits and acquaintances. In mid-September, he continued, alone, to Trieste, Venice and Verona (from where he wrote a last postcard to Bauer) and then went to a sanatorium in Riva that he knew from an earlier stay.

In Riva, Kafka made the acquaintance of the 'Swiss woman', a girl of 18. This was, after the *Zuckmantel* (Zlaté hory) experience eight years earlier, his second taste of that 'sweetness in a relationship with a woman one loves'.[7] Kafka 'for the first time understood a Christian girl and lived almost entirely within the sphere of her influence',[8] though this time 'she was half a child and I was altogether confused and sick in every possible way'.[9] Almost ten years later, he still spoke of the 'peaceful numbness'[10] of those days. As with the encounter in *Zuckmantel*, hardly anything is known about this liaison: Kafka strictly observed 'her commandment not to mention her'.[11] Three and a half years later, he paid clear homage to this love affair by setting his story 'The Hunter Gracchus' in Riva. ('Gracchus' is one of Kafka's many codes for himself: in Czech 'kavka' means 'jackdaw', which in Italian is 'gracchio'.)

'Perhaps I have caught hold of myself again',[12] Kafka wrote in his diary after his return from Riva. Two weeks later, he resumed his correspondence with Bauer and visited her in November. A Prague friend, the writer Ernst Weiss, and a friend of Bauer's, Grete Bloch, acted as mediators. In May 1914, Felice Bauer came to Prague, a flat was rented, and on 1 June the official engagement took place in Berlin. It was a 'rescue attempt': even in March, Kafka recorded in his diary that the breach of the preceding year had been caused by concern 'over my literary work ... for I thought marriage would jeopardise it'.[13] His hope of 'literary work' had not been fulfilled over the past few months: 'I cannot wait in double hopelessness: I cannot see F. more and more slipping from my grasp, and myself more and more unable to escape.'[14] Engagement did not bring the hoped-for release from this disability: he felt 'tied hand and foot like a criminal, set down in a corner bound in chains'.[15] Just 18 days before (!) his engagement, Kafka had reminded Bauer's friend Grete Bloch of an inauspicious episode in the life of Grillparzer.*

---

*The Viennese dramatist Franz Grillparzer (1791–1872) was important to Kafka

The engagement had been broken off ages ago, only the most half-witted relatives still believed in some faint possibility of a marriage, by which time Katharina was well over 30. One evening G. [Grillparzer] goes to see the sisters, as he does most evenings; K. is particularly nice to him, partly out of pity he makes her sit on his lap – the two sisters are presumably walking around the room – whereupon he discovers, and later writes it down, that he feels utterly indifferent to K., that at the time he had had to force himself that he would have been glad to have experienced the slightest emotion, but that he had no alternative but to keep her on his lap and then after a while to extricate himself again. Incidentally, it wasn't just pity that made him take her on his lap, it was almost a test; worse, he foresaw the consequences, yet did it. [16]

On 12 July – two weeks after the assassination of Archduke Franz Ferdinand in Sarajevo – Kafka broke off the engagement in Berlin, travelled to the Baltic Sea (accompanied for some of the trip by Ernst Weiss) and on 26 July, three days after Austria's ultimatum to Serbia, returned to Prague.

Because of his weak constitution, Kafka was exempted from military service. As for the world war, there are barely 50 lines about it in his letters or his diary. His views are unequivocal: he speaks 'of envy, and hatred against those who are fighting and to whom I

---

less for his plays than for his diaries and his short story 'The Poor Minstrel' (1848). The latter focuses on an amateur violinist whose art compensates for his failure in love and work; though dedicated to his art, he is grotesquely bad at it, but plays for God alone and puts up serenely with poverty and ridicule. Grillparzer's diaries reveal the frustrations he endured as a reluctant bureaucrat (director of the Vienna court archive) and record his relationship with Katharina (Kathi) Fröhlich, to whom he was engaged but whom he could never resolve to marry.

Kafka's sisters Valli (left) and Elli, 1910.

passionately wish everything evil'. [17] A mere eight days after the out-break of the war, he noted in his diary: 'Patriotic parade ... These parades are one of the most disgusting accompaniments of the war ... I stand there with my malignant look.' [18] This look is the same *malignant* or – allowing for Kafka's excessive self-criticism – the same neutral, cool, matter-of-fact look as that of the traveller in *In the Penal Colony* (written two months later) who, as an honoured guest in a prison colony, learns that it is customary to torture delin-quents to death by inscribing on their body the command they have violated and wonders whether he has any right to condemn an unfa-miliar practice, however barbarous it may seem.

In August, Kafka had to give up his flat in his parents' house *Niklasstraße* 36 (Mikuláška, now Pařížska třída) because his eldest sister was moving there with her two children for the duration of the war. So it was not until the age of 31 – and then only because he had to – that Kafka left his supposedly unbearable family circle. He lived at first in the flat of his sister Valli at *Bilekgasse* 10 (Bílkova), then in that of his sister Elli at *Nerudagasse* 48 (Nerudova, now Polská), and only in February 1915 rented a room of his own, again in *Bilekgasse* 10. Within a month, however, he gave it up in order to move into *Lange Gasse* 18 (Dlouhá trida), which is now 16, the house 'At the Golden Pike'. In 1917 Kafka moved once more, this time into an apartment in the Schönborn Palace.

The dissolution of his engagement, the outbreak of war, and leaving his parental home at last gave Kafka the solitude he had both longed for and feared. A few days later, he noted in his diary: 'My talent for portraying my dreamlike inner life has thrust all other matters into the background; my life has dwindled dreadfully, nor will it cease to dwindle. Nothing will ever satisfy me.'[19] It was at this point, after a pause of a year and a half, that a new creative period began:

> I have been writing these past few days, may it continue. Today I am not so completely protected by and enclosed in my work as I was two years ago, nevertheless I have the feeling that my monotonous, empty, mad bachelor's life has some justification. I can once more carry on a conversation with myself and don't stare so into complete emptiness. Only in this way is there any possibility of improvement for me.[20]

That month, August 1914, Kafka began to write *The Trial*. The novel is *also* an autobiographical punishment fantasy: Josef K is killed *on the eve of his 31st birthday*; on the eve of his own 31st birthday, Kafka had decided to travel to Berlin to break off his engagement with Bauer. In his diary, Kafka called the breach of the engagement, in the Askanischer Hof Hotel, 'the law-court in the hotel'.[21] By then, of course, the Habsburg heir to the throne and his wife had been assassinated. As an Austro-Hungarian subject, Kafka

Manuscript page of *The Trial*.

drew this parallel in his diary, while engaged in writing *The Trial*: 'The thoughts provoked in me by the war resemble my old worries about F. in the agonising way in which they gnaw at me from so many different sides.' [22]

Again, Kafka writes very quickly: several chapters are finished within two months. At the beginning of October he takes a week's leave to 'push the novel on'. [23] After three days he interrupted his work on *The Trial*, extended his vacation by another week, and during those 10 nights between 8 and 18 October wrote the final chapter of *Amerika* and *In the Penal Colony* – in all, nearly 70 printed pages.

At the heart of Kafka's vision in *The Trial* is the enigmatic story of the doorkeeper, in which a man wastes his life, hesitating to enter a door that offers access to the Law, until, just as he is about to die, he is told that the door was destined specially for him. (In his diary, Kafka calls it a 'legend', in the novel a 'story', found 'in the introductory writings to the law'.) [24] A doorkeeper already appears in the first sketch of the novel (of 29 July 1914). It is not only one of Kafka's most famous stories, but also one of those he liked best. He later lifted it from the chapter 'In the Cathedral' in *The Trial* and called it 'Before the Law'. He often read it to friends (including to Felice Bauer a few months later) and placed it in the volume of short stories (most of them, with one exception, written later) entitled *A Country Doctor*.*

In October 1914, Kafka's diary contains increasingly frequent entries such as 'No work done. Almost completely at a standstill. Today nothing again'. Kafka was scarcely able to work at night as he had to spend his afternoons supervising the factory of his brother-in-law, who had been called up for military service. As in the autumn of 1913, and again as 'a rescue attempt', his thoughts returned to Felice Bauer:

> Before me lies the office and [work in] the factory that is going down. But I am totally at a loss. And my strongest support, strangely enough, is thinking of F.... I have now lived calmly for two months without any real contact with F., have dreamed of F.

---

* *The Trial*. On his 30th birthday, the banker Josef K, a high-achieving, workaholic bachelor, is arrested in his bedroom by two guards who wear an unrecognisable uniform and claim to represent an unheard-of court. Without asking what he is charged with, he defiantly asserts his innocence and proclaims his disregard for the court. Yet the court turns out to have premises in attics and concealed corridors throughout the city; it seems able to read K's thoughts; it punishes the misbehaviour of K's guards by having them brutally flogged, but its officials are vain, licentious and corrupt; and genuine acquittals by the court are recorded only in legends. K's uncle tells him: 'To be prosecuted in a case like this means that one has already lost it.' Though he hires a lawyer, K is more interested in the help he might receive from the various women he encounters, and he also hopes for advice from the court painter and the prison chaplain; but neither the ambiguous art of the painter, nor the parable of the doorkeeper which the chaplain tells him, enable K to avert his death at the hands of the court's executioners.

Passport photograph taken at about the time Kafka wrote *The Trial*.

as though of someone who was dead and could never live again, and now, when I am offered a chance to come near her, she is at once the centre of everything again. And now I completely balk at any work. Yet it isn't balking; I see the task and the way to it, I simply have to push small obstacles, but cannot do it. Reply from Bl. arrived; I am completely undecided as to how to answer it.[25]

Bl. was Grete Bloch, Felice Bauer's friend, with whom Kafka had been corresponding since the spring of 1914; it was through her that Kafka had been 'offered a chance' of resuming contact with Bauer. He hesitated at first, but an extensive correspondence with Grete Bloch soon developed, becoming, it seems, a relationship intimate enough to play a part in the dissolution of his engagement to Felice Bauer. It is not known how far it went. According to a letter from

Grete Bloch, Felice Bauer's friend and the intermediary between Kafka and his fiancée. She became very close to Kafka, even talking about a child she bore him in one of her letters.

Grete Bloch, dating from 1940, she bore him a son in 1915, who died seven years later, even before Kafka. However, this seems to be a mystification; no evidence of Kafka's paternity has been discovered despite intensive efforts to do so. The role played by Grete Bloch (as 'judge'[26]) in the end of Kafka's engagement remains uncertain. It is also unclear whether Kafka was planning a visit before or only after the break-up to Gleschendorf near the Baltic. What is certain is that only a telephone call shortly before his visit made him change his plan; instead he travelled to Marienlyst in Denmark, meeting up with Ernst Weiss in Lübeck.

The 'pattern' of 1915 followed entirely that of 1913. During its first few months some pages were written, as well as the fragment 'Blumfeld, an Elderly Bachelor'; after that Kafka's creativity dried up once more for the next year and a half. In January, Kafka met Felice Bauer for the first time since the break-up in *Bodenbach* (Podmokly). He commented:

We found each other quite unchanged in other ways as well.

Each of us silently says to himself that the other is immovable
and merciless. I yield not a particle of my demand for a fantastic
life arranged solely in the interest of my work; she, indifferent
to every mute request, wants the average: a comfortable home,
an interest on my part in the factory, good food, bed at 11,
central heating; sets my watch – which for the past three
months has been an hour and a half fast – right to the minute.
And she is right in the end; she is right when she corrects the
bad German I used to the waiter, and I can put nothing right
when she speaks of the 'personal touch' (it cannot be said any
way but gratingly) in the furnishings she intends to have in her
home.[27]

This time Kafka viewed his relationship with Bauer noticeably
more coolly. He did not, especially at a time without literary inspiration, wish to continue his, to him nonsensical, life in the same
way as before. Felice Bauer was a way out. A second, rather strange,
'escape attempt' was his application to do military service: at first in
December 1915 arguing his case orally and then in May 1916 apply-
ing officially in writing to the Insurance Institute. His diary gives a
very different account of his reasons:

And so gave the letter to the Director ... Asked either for a long
leave later on, without pay of course, in the event of the war
ending by autumn; or, if the war goes on, for my exemption
[from military service] to be cancelled. It was a complete lie. It
would have been half a lie if I had asked for a long leave at once,
and, if it were refused, for my dismissal. It would have been the
truth if had given notice.
  Pointless discussion today. The Director thought I wanted
to extort three weeks' holiday, which in my exempted status I
am not entitled to ... He seemed to find a long leave without

pay funny, curiously referred to it in that tone ... Remarkably enough, he did not speak of my writing.[28]

The application was refused and Kafka did not refer to it again, since a few months later the original conditions for this 'escape attempt' no longer pertained. In July 1916, Kafka spent ten days with Bauer at the Hotel Balmoral and Osborne in *Marienbad* (Mariánské Lázné). Until that moment, for almost four years he had had for her only 'unlimited admiration, humility, sympathy, despair and self-contempt';[29] and even during the first few days in *Marienbad* there is still talk of 'the hardships of living together ... and only deep down, perhaps, a thin little stream worthy of the name of love ... Intolerable living with anyone. I don't regret this; I regret the impossibility for me of not living alone.'[30] But a few days later we suddenly read: 'I had been intimate with F. only in letters, in human terms only for the past two days. But it's not that clear, doubts remain. But beautiful the glance of her calmed eyes, the opening-up of womanly depth.'[31] And after Bauer's departure, Kafka wrote to Brod:

Since things could not have become worse, they took a turn for the better. The cords with which I was trussed were at least somewhat loosened; I straightened out somewhat while she who had constantly been holding out her hands to help but reaching only into an outer void, helped again and we arrived at a human relationship of a kind ... But now I saw the look of trustfulness in a woman's eyes, and I could not fail to respond. Much has been torn open that I wanted to shield forever (I am not speaking of anything in particular but of the whole); and through this rent will come, I know, enough unhappiness for more than a lifetime, but this unhappiness is nothing summoned up, but rather imposed. I have no right to shirk it, especially since, if what is happening were not happening, I

would of my own accord make it happen, simply to have her
turn that look upon me ... Now all that has changed and is good.
Our agreement is in brief to get married soon after the end of
the war, to rent an apartment of two or three rooms in some
Berlin suburb, and each to assume economic responsibilities for
himself F. will go on working as she has done all along, while I –
well, for myself I cannot yet say.[32]

This *agreement*, an informal second engagement, nevertheless
gave Kafka a new sense of security – quite unlike that of the spring of
1914 – and his productivity also returned gradually. Meanwhile, his
work began to be known by a wider circle. In the late autumn of 1915,
the highly successful dramatist Carl Sternheim passed on to Kafka
the prize money he had received with the literary Fontane Prize.

The Metamorphosis appeared in November 1915 as a double
volume (22/23) of the *Day of Judgement* series, and *The Judgement*
as volume 34 in September 1916. On 10 November, Kafka gave his
second (and last) public reading: in the Munich Goltz bookshop
he read his story 'In the Penal Colony'. Felice Bauer was present.
According to reports from his audience, his method of recitation
matched his prose – cool, unadorned, without the declamatory his-
trionics then fashionable, and with a hard 'Prague-German' accent.

'I returned from Munich with renewed courage',[33] he later wrote.
He had already sought out a new flat, since his time in *Marienbad*;
the one on *Lange Gasse* (Dlouhá) was, as always, too noisy: 'My
neighbour talks for hours with the landlady. Both speak softly, the
landlady almost inaudibly, and therefore so much the worse ... Is it
like this in every house? ... From time to time a crash in the kitchen
or the corridor. Yesterday, in the attic above, perpetual rolling of a
ball, as someone for some incomprehensible reason were bowling,
then a piano below me in addition.'[34]

Whenever Kafka thought that his inner situation allowed him

to write, he very quickly managed to create the external conditions: he accepted his sister Ottla's offer to work in the evenings and at night in the house that she rented in the *Alchimistengasse* 22 (Zlatá ulička) on *Hradshin* (Hradčany), one of the minute houses (really just a single room) which, in the late Middle Ages, had been built into the curve of the castle wall to accommodate the castle guards. Kafka wrote:

> It had all the defects of a house newly occupied ... Today it suits me perfectly. In every respect: the pleasant walk up to the house, the silence ... I take my evening meal up there, and usually remain there until midnight; and then the advantage of the walk home: I have to remind myself to stop, then I have the walk to cool my head. As for life there, it is something very special to have a house of one's own, to keep the world out by locking the door – not of a room, not of an apartment, but of a house; to step out of the front door directly into the snow and the quiet street.[35]

During that winter of 1916/17, Kafka wrote almost all the stories in the collection *A Country Doctor*, plus several more. Most of these he wrote in pencil in eight octavo notebooks, which have survived. The first of these contains the stories: 'A Country Doctor', 'Up in the Gallery', 'A Fratricide', 'The Next Village', 'The Bridge', 'The Hunter Gracchus', 'The Bucket Rider', 'Jackals and Arabs', 'The New Advocate' and the dramatic fragment 'The Warden of the Tomb'.

In March 1917, Kafka rented a two-room apartment in the Schönborn Palace so that he could, at long last, give up his room in the *Lange Gasse*, stop disturbing his sister every evening, and provide Bauer with an opportunity, after their planned marriage at the end of the war, to recuperate in Prague for a few months.

This palace, built in the 18th century for the family of the Counts of Schönborn, is situated on the *Kleinseite* (Malá strana), with a large garden extending to the lower flank of the *Laurenziberg* (Petřín hill). There, and partly still at his sister's house in the *Alchimisten-gasse*, Kafka continued his entries in the octavo notebooks. On the first few pages of one of these octavo notebooks begins the longish story 'The Great Wall of China', very clearly inspired by a historic site in Prague in the immediate vicinity of Kafka's apartment. The Hunger Wall on *Laurenziberg*, a wall with no purpose at all, built to provide employment for unemployed workers and the destitute. Like the Hunger Wall, Kafka's Great Wall is built only in sections. As soon as one section is completed, the workmen are sent to a remote region to build another section, so that the observer must conclude that the command deliberately 'chose the system of piecemeal con-struction. But the piecemeal construction was only a makeshift and therefore inexpedient. Remains the conclusion that the command willed something inexpedient.'[36]

Kafka developed these themes of official *inexpediency* and point-lessness in the parable 'An Imperial Message', which he later lifted from its context and, along with the story 'An Old Manuscript' (which has a similar subject), included in the volume *A Country Doctor*. While in the Schönborn Palace and in the *Alchimisten-gasse*, he also wrote 'The Knock at the Manor Gate', 'A Report to the Academy', and two stories about his own writing: 'Eleven Sons' (a characterisation of 11 stories that he had written during the pre-ceding months) and 'The Cares of a Family Man', which can be interpreted as a confession of anxiety about the story 'The Hunter Gracchus', on which he had worked for many weeks without ever completing it.

Kafka's new 'self-assurance' emerged most clearly in his decision to become engaged to Felice officially. At the beginning of July, Felice came to Prague. Max Brod reports on the 'pitiful sight'[37] that Kafka presented at the conventional round of calls (on which Bauer

Kafka and Felice Bauer in Budapest, 1917.

presumably insisted). In mid-July, he travelled with Felice to visit her sister Erna in Hungary. Four days previously he had sent his publisher Kurt Wolff the manuscript of the volume *A Country Doctor* as 'some of the more useful work from this period' (the winter); as he intended to 'give up [his] job' and marry, he hoped that Kurt Wolff would not quite desert him[38] – on which Wolff immediately put his mind at rest. At the same time, Kafka got *In the Penal Colony* ready for the press, having once more reworked the conclusion of the story. This time he was evidently determined to give up his employment, get married, and live solely as a writer.

A few days after his return from Hungary, at the beginning of August 1917, Kafka recorded coughing up blood – this was the beginning of pulmonary tuberculosis, diagnosed a month later. For five years, he had struggled against his civil service job, against – and at times for – being bound by matrimony, according to the strength of his fluctuating sense of literary calling. Now he wrote in his octavo notebook: 'For the eventuality that in the near future I may die or become wholly unfit to live ... let me say that I myself have torn myself to shreds ... The world – F. is its representative – and my ego are tearing my body apart in a conflict that there is no resolving.'[39]

A few weeks later, he wrote in his diary: 'It is the age of the wound rather than its depth and festering which makes it painful.'[40]

8

The Wound

KAFKA ALWAYS REGARDED THE 'WOUND' as 'punishment' and a 'symbol'. In a letter from September 1917, he himself reminded Brod of the 'incurable open wound' in *A Country Doctor*,[1] of which, the wounded young man declares, 'A fine wound is all I brought into the world; that was my sole endowment'. The country doctor, trying to console him, declares that it is '"Not so bad ... Many a one proffers his side and can hardly hear the axe in the forest, far less that it is coming nearer to him."'[2]

Three years later he would write to Milena Jesenská:

What happened was that the brain could no longer endure the burden of worry and suffering heaped upon it. It said: 'I give up; but should there be someone still interested in the maintenance of the whole, then he must relieve me of some of my burden and things will still go on for a while.' Then the lung spoke up, though it probably hadn't much to lose anyhow. These discussions between brain and lung, which went on without my knowledge, may have been terrible.[3]

Nevertheless, Kafka evidently felt a certain satisfaction that 'the disease which has been being summoned for years now has suddenly

Zürau (Siřem).

broken out. It is almost a relief',[4] he wrote to Kurt Wolff. According-ing to another testimony, Kafka declared just one day after return-ing from Budapest (before the outbreak of the disease), 'that he had broken with his fiancée. He was entirely calm when he said this. He even seemed to feel well.'[5] It was a release from all the responsibili-ties (office, marital obligations, his parents) that for many years he had believed he must undertake. For the first time he took eight months' leave from the Insurance Institute and went to *Zürau* (Siřem), a small village in north-western Bohemia, where his sister Ottla was managing a farm belonging to her brother-in-law. A few days later he wrote to Brod:

> ... freedom, freedom above all. However there is still the wound
> of which the lesions in the lung are only the symbol ... You
> misunderstand it, Max. but perhaps I also misunderstand it

and there is no understanding these things ... because there is no seeing it whole, so turbulent and ever-moving is the gigantic mass which yet at the same time never ceases to grow. Misery, misery, but what is it but our own nature? And if the misery were ultimately to be disentangled (perhaps only women can do such work), you and I would fall apart.

In any case, my attitude towards the tuberculosis today resembles that of a child clinging to the pleats of its mother's skirts ... I am constantly seeking an explanation for this disease, for I did not seek it. Sometimes it seems to me that my brain and lungs came to an agreement without my knowledge ...

But ... put in these terms the whole thing is totally wrong. The first step to insight. The first step on the stairway which culminates in a made-up marital bed as the reward and meaning of my human existence (which however would then have been well-nigh Napoleonic). The bed will never be made up and I, that is my destiny, shall never leave Corsica behind me ...

Should I give thanks that I have not been able to marry? I would then have become all at once what I am now becoming gradually: mad. With shorter and shorter periods of remission – during which not I but It gathers strength.[6]

On 20 September, Felice Bauer visited Kafka in *Zürau*: 'I myself am unable to take hold of myself I am as helpless as I am unfeeling ... I am guilty of the wrong for which she is tortured, and what is more, I am wielding the instrument of torture',[7] he noted in his diary. In Prague, towards the end of December 1917 the couple finally dissolved their engagement, Bauer having gone there from Berlin and Kafka from *Zürau*. On 27 December, Bauer returned to Berlin: immediately afterwards Kafka went to see Brod at his office: 'He had just been to the station to see off F.,' Brod writes.

His face was pale, hard and severe. But suddenly he began to cry. It was the only time I saw him cry. I shall never forget the scene, it is one of the most terrible I have ever experienced. I was not sitting alone in my office; right close up to my desk was the desk of a colleague – we worked in the legal section of the general post office ... proper, dusty, ugly, impersonal office premises ... Kafka had come straight into the room I worked in to see me, in the middle of all the office work, sat near my desk on a small chair which stood there ready for bearers of petitions, pensioners and debtors. And in this place he was crying, in this place he said between his sobs: 'Is it not terrible that such a thing must happen?' The tears were streaming down his cheeks. I have never except this once seen him upset quite without control of himself.[8]

This deep distress cannot be explained by Kafka's conclusion that, as a person suffering from tuberculosis, he could not marry; on the contrary, he had virtually brought on the outbreak of the disease in order to *free* himself. (Medical textbooks list this as one of the possible causes of the disease.) The disease was only the pretext for his break with Bauer; this emerges from a letter to Ottla, written the following day, which once more reveals how devastated he was:

The days with F. were bad (aside from the first day, when we had not yet talked about the main thing), and on the last morning I wept more than in all my years after childhood. But of course it would have been much worse, or impossible, if I had had the least shred of a doubt as to the rightness of what I was doing. There was nothing of the sort, though alas the rightness of an action is no less right when this action is wrong and became all the more a wrong by the calmness and especially by the kindness with which she received it ...

The official reason for cancelling the engagement is solely the disease; that is how I've put it to Father also.[9]

For Kafka, his months in *Zürau* were an experiment, an attempt to break with everything – with Felice Bauer, with the office, with Prague and with his father. Ottla, his youngest sister, nine years his junior, supported him in this. Whereas in earlier years he had believed that he had 'really kept her down'[10] after 1916 a more intimate relationship developed between them: 'Ottla understands many things, even a great many'[11] about his situation. He frequently read to her (Dostoevsky, Schopenhauer and Kleist, as well as his own work), supported her in her plans, often took her along on his trips, and during his final years frequently stayed with her, not only in *Zürau*, but also in *Planá* (1922) and in *Schelesen* (Želízy) (1923).

Along with Max Brod (and for a shorter period Milena Jesenská) Ottla was the only person from whom Kafka had no secrets. Their mother's characteristics were 'impossible to discern'[12] in her. Of the three sisters, she was the one most similar to their father: she had continual arguments with him and later married on her own decision – her two sisters 'were' married.

Kafka described her as 'pure, truthful, honest, consistent. Humility and pride, sympathetic understanding and distance, devotion and independence, vision and courage in unerring balance'[13] – though the passive traits among these were probably more her mother's inheritance. The two siblings' relationship, admittedly, was also one directed **against** their father. Thus, Kafka, during a short stay in Prague, reported to Ottla in *Zürau*:

> Yesterday there was again a great fuss in the evening, although it didn't go on for long. The old business … Zürau, that crazy girl deserting her poor parents; what kind of work could there be out there now? Fine to be in the country where everything is to

Kafka and his sister
Ottla in *Zürau*, 1917/18.

be had in abundance; but she ought to go hungry for once and
have real troubles, etc. ...

All this was, of course, indirectly aimed at me; here and there
this actually came out in the open; they said I had backed up
or been to blame for this abnormal behaviour, etc (to which I
responded not badly or at least unanswerably that abnormal
behaviour was not the worst thing because normality was, for
instance, the World War) ...

As the result of these conversations it now appears to
my somewhat freshly opened eyes that you or I are almost
completely in the right as against these worries and reproaches,
in the right insofar as we are 'ungrateful' and have 'deserted' our
parents, insofar as we are 'crazy'. For we have neither deserted
them nor are we ungrateful or crazy, rather with sufficiently

decent intentions we have done what we considered necessary and what nobody (in order, say, to relieve us of the burden) could have done for us. Father has only one real basis for reproach, namely, that we have everything too easy (no matter whether this is to his credit or his blame). He knows no other test except that of hunger, money worries, and perhaps sickness. He recognises that we have not yet passed the first of these tests, which without doubt are powerful; and so he is entitled to forbid us every free word. There is some truth to this, and because it is true some goodness, too. As long as we cannot do without his help in keeping hunger and money worries at bay, our conduct to him remains constrained and we must yield to him in some way, even we do not do it outwardly. In this realm something more than the father speaks with his voice, more than the merely non-loving father ...

This letter was already in the envelope when I asked Mother about her worries. So it turns out I am the worry after all; Father was so inconsiderate as to tell her everything.[14]

Between 1917 and 1919, relations between Kafka and his father deteriorated. Kafka supported Ottla in her agricultural plans (which their father regarded as 'crazy'), helped her in the search for an agricultural college and arranged for her to be accepted as a student. For a long time, Kafka concealed his illness from his father, finally giving it as the reason for the breaking off of the engagement. (His father had thought that Bauer, unlike all Kafka's other women, was the right choice.) These were the first symptoms of the argument that two years later culminated in the 'Letter to his Father'.

In *Zürau*, Kafka examined the results of his *liberation attempts*. Three weeks after the move he noted in his diary: 'I can still have passing satisfaction from works like *A Country Doctor*, provided I can still write such things at all (very improbable). But happiness only if I can raise the world into the pure, the true and the immutable.'[15] He produced no narrative works during his time in *Zürau* (with the – extremely characteristic – exceptions of the brief 'parables' *A Common Confusion*: 'The Truth about Sancho Panza', 'The Silence of the Sirens' and 'Prometheus'). Instead he wrote the famous 109 *aphorisms*, excerpted from a multitude of notes. For a long time, philosophical problems eclipsed everything else: Kafka was reading several works of Kierkegaard and the *Confessions* of Saint Augustine. With his friend Oskar Baum, who visited him for a week, he discussed the views of Tolstoy. Into this period also falls the beginning of his studies of Hebrew. It also seems as if the concept of *The Castle* – which was not written until over four years later – dates back to that winter in *Zürau*, as a diary entry mentions an intention to write a planned novel.[16] He was clearly impressed by the peasant life, which he encountered there for the first time and described in numerous notes. In the same diary entry he observed: 'General impression given one by peasants: noblemen who have escaped into agriculture, where they have arranged their work so wisely and humbly that it fits perfectly into everything and they are protected against all insecurity and worry until their blissful death. True dwellers on this earth.'[17]

His struggle for the 'happiness [to] raise the world into the pure, the true, and the immutable' foundered in *Zürau*. It is therefore highly questionable to take this quotation as centrally emblematic of Kafka's thought in general (as opposed to his ideals). Likewise, the famous quote about *writing as a form of prayer* (which Kafka wrote in the late autumn of 1920, while preparing a fair copy of his aphorisms on separate sheets, giving occasion to reflect again on his time in the Zürau) is always being cited only partially and taken out of context; it is followed by a telling remark: *writing as a form of prayer. Difference between Zürau and Prague. Didn't I put up enough of a struggle then?* At the end of June 1918, some time after his return to Prague, he said to Brod: 'One must confine oneself to what one absolutely masters.' To which Brod notes in his diary: 'country vs. city. Better here though, he was just frittering his time away in Zürau ... wants to keep himself quite pure.'[18] Kafka realised just as happiness was not possible in Prague, neither was *purity*. But, typically, nearly all the (extant) narrative works of the next few years were written during the interim stays in Prague.

It is exceedingly doubtful whether Kafka ever genuinely wanted to leave his home city. Yet his desire for isolation and *purity* were a kind of response to the outside world: without it, they became meaningless. Time and again over the next six years, Kafka cut short his numerous stays in sanatoria, often in a way that looks like an escape. Nor were his intervening stays in Prague merely attempts to prove himself capable of work at the Insurance Institute. Even after his retirement, Kafka spent half of his remaining 23 months in Prague. Kafka did not wish to be cured completely – not simply in order to punish himself, but because total isolation from the world around him would have simultaneously rendered any reaction to it impossible.

During summer and autumn 1918, Kafka remained in Prague, except for two short visits to *Rumburg* (Rumburk) and *Turnau* (Trnov). In November he went to *Schelesen* (Želízy), a small village north of Prague (at Liboch on the River Elbe), where he stayed until the spring at the *Pension Stüdl*. There he made the acquaintance of Julie Wohryzek, a young Czech girl, the daughter of a shoemaker and custodian at the *Weinberge* (Vinohrady) synagogue in Prague. Again he abandoned his intention of 'shutting himself off'. A mere year and a half after breaking off his engagement to Bauer, and just six months after meeting Julie Wohryzek, Kafka became engaged for a third time. The speed of his decision suggests that this time he was confident he had made a good choice. 'It might have become a marriage of reason in the best sense of the word',[19] he later wrote.

Pension Stüdl in *Schelesen*, where, in November
1919, Kafka wrote 'Letter to his Father'.

Little is known about this engagement – his letters to Julie Wohryzek are lost – until a lengthy letter from Kafka to Wohryzek's sister
Käthe was found in 1963. Written after his breach with Wohryzek
in November 1919, it describes the prelude to the engagement and
its history:

You know how J. and I met. The beginning of this acquaintance

was very odd and, for superstitious people, not exactly
promising of happiness. For a few days we laughed continuously
whenever we met one another, at meals, on walks, when sitting
opposite each other. Basically, this laughter was not pleasant,
it was without obvious reason, it was tormenting, shaming.
It contributed to the fact that we kept more away from one
another, gave up meals together, and saw each other more rarely.
This, I believe, was in line with our general intention. Although
(apart from illness) I had a relatively happy, free and quiet year
behind me I was still only like a wounded person, who lives
tolerably so long as he does not knock into anything, but who,
at the first touch at the right spot, is thrown back to the worst
initial pains – not as the old experiences were reviving again, no,
those are and remain in the past, but the formal aspect of pain
has remained, rather like an old wound ... in which the new pain
immediately drives up and down, terrible as on the first day and
more terrible because one has become so much less resistant ...
For me it was then like this even during the first days, one of the
first nights was my first sleepless night for a year. I understood
the threat.

It was perhaps easier for J., both as a girl and also because she
has a wonderful mixture of warmth and coolness that is hard to
upset from outside.

So we managed it, though we had recuperated very little, I in
particular would have much preferred to see a doctor every day
with my heart, but we managed it. We had established between
us that, in a certain sense, I regarded marriage and children as
the highest desirable goal on earth, but that I could not possibly
marry (proof of this, as all the rest proved too unintelligible,
were my two broken engagements) and that we therefore had to
part. Which is what happened.

In point of fact, we did not once write to each other during the three weeks I stayed alone in Schelesen, but when I got to Prague we flew towards each other as if driven. There was no other possibility, not for either of us. Admittedly, on the face of it I was in a position to determine how things turned out ...

What then were the resistances within me, which refused to go away, despite everything, which were, in a sense, lurking and watching developments? I can truly speak about them as about something alien because they far exceed my personal strength and I am, if you like, totally in their power. To begin with, material worries are entirely excluded ... It is something different, something speaks to me, mixing material worries, which in themselves are of little consequence, with devilish cunning among the others: You, who have to fight ceaselessly for your inner survival, with all the strength you have and this is not even sufficient, you want to set up your own home life ... With what strength are you going to accomplish this? And you want to have as many children as will be given to you, because you are marrying in order to become a better person than you are, and you shy away in horror from any limitation of children in marriage. But you are not a peasant whose children are nourished by the land, nor are you, at bottom, a businessman, I mean by inner inclination, but rather a civil servant (probably a pariah class of the European professional man), at the same time excessively nervous, profoundly lost to all the dangers of literature, with a weak lung, unhappily shirking the little writing work at the office. With these preconditions (readily admitting that marriage is a must) you want to marry? Moreover you have the temerity to demand, with such intentions, that you sleep at night without on the following days running about as on fire, half maddened by headaches? And with such a wedding present you wish to make a trusting, devoted, unbelievably unselfish girl happy? ...

Julie Wohryzek, Kafka's second fiancée.

At first all these major reservations hide away in the face of your firm resolve; though they attempt to shake it with all the torments of sleeplessness, they dare not, for a long time, emerge in their true shape. That was what I built my hope on. The whole thing was a race between the external facts and my internal weakness. There were several phases, first a delay due to medical examination while my professor was on vacation – that was bad; then the opposition of my father, which did not last too long – that was good, also because it distracted me and diverted my thoughts from the actual dangers; next came the opportunity of a tolerable immediate apartment – now that was excellent, a short hasty week, the banns were assured, we would have been married. But on Friday it emerged that, since the apartment had eluded us, we could not be married on Sunday. I am not flying to say that this was a disaster, maybe an

Hermann Kafka, 1910.

even worse collapse would have come later and would then have buried a married couple. All I am trying to say is that my hope of achieving matrimony was not unjustified and that, judged by the facts, I myself was a poor person and, because of poverty, dependent on gambling, but I was not a liar.

That was then the turning point, later it was no longer to be stopped, the time granted me had run out, what until then had been a warning from afar was now really thundering in my ears day and night. J. knew from outward signs roughly how it was; in the end I could not continue and had to tell her.[20]

Once more the same pattern: the *internal compulsion* to enforce a marriage *through extreme, unsparing effort* – a few months later he said: 'It was exclusively me who had urged this marriage, she had only complied, frightened and resisting'[21] – even though he knew how *rash* this was, especially after the outbreak of his disease. Time and again Kafka tried to meet the *demands* of the world. What he

First edition of *In the Penal Colony*, 1919.

regarded as 'the world' kept switching between the archetypes of office work to father to wife – but it was always in opposition to his writing. It is misleading to interpret this pattern medically – as has been done – or to speak of Kafka's 'impotence' (from which he did not suffer either early or late in life, as is amply documented) instead of his purism. Equally, it would be wrong to point to his 'father complex'. This complex certainly existed, but it would more fittingly be described as a 'world complex'. The centrality of this pattern is clear, more than at any other time, in November 1919, when Kafka wrote not only the letter to Julie Wohryzek's sister quoted above, but also the 'Letter to his Father' – again from *Schelesen*, where he had returned for a few weeks after living in Prague from spring until autumn. Indeed, even though there are no diary entries relating to this period, they would probably, as usual, have contained remarks about how unbearable office work was; as it is, there is no shortage of such material in the 'Letter to his Father'.

So-called 'medical' or 'psychological' discussions of Kafka's

'Letter to his Father' tend to obscure the extent to which Kafka was quite justified in complaining about his father's rudeness and inconsiderateness at this time. When *In the Penal Colony* was published in October 1919, Kafka (as he had done with all his previous works) presented his father with a copy.* As always happened on such occasions, Kafka senior, annoyed at having his evening game of cards interrupted, gave the curt response: 'Put it on my bedside table!'[22] What may have been no more than carelessness became calculated rudeness when he was informed of his son's engagement to Julie Wohryzek. He objected most violently to this liaison, which, in his eyes, would be a disgrace to his 'name'.[23] In the class scheme of the Jewish bourgeoisie, Wohryzek's father, a synagogue custodian, was on the lowest rung. His father's invective, as reported by Kafka, concluded with the advice that Kafka – by then 36 years of age – would do better to go to a brothel:

> She probably put on a fancy blouse, something these Prague Jewesses are good at, and right away, of course, you decided to marry her. And that as fast as possible, in a week, tomorrow, today. I can't understand you. After all, you're a grown man, you live in the city, and you don't know what to do but marry the next best girl. Isn't there anything else you can do? If you are frightened, I'll go with you.[24]

Such is the background to the 'Letter to his Father', the most painful and opaque autobiographical document, in which Kafka,

---

*Kurt Tucholsky on *In the Penal Colony*: 'This slim book, a wonderful Drugulin Press publication, is a masterpiece ... Don't ask what it is driving at. It's not driving at anything. It doesn't mean anything. Perhaps the book does not even belong in our age; certainly it does not get us any further. It has no problems and it knows no doubts or questions. It is quite harmless. As harmless as Kleist.' (*Die Weltbühne*, 1920)

outraged by disrespect and oppression, presents some aspects of his life in an undeniably distorted form.

In December 1919, Kafka returned to Prague and stayed there until the beginning of April 1920. He never sent or handed over the 'Letter to his Father'. While in Prague he tried once more to present his situation – in aphorisms which pose as universal statements but which use a 'He' character that admittedly in several places still clearly derives from an 'I' or blur into it. The second of the aphorisms reveals how little anonymity, in the strict sense of the word, there actually is in this He: 'He found the Archimedean point, but used it against himself. It seems that he was only permitted to find it under this condition.' At another point, the reference to the basic pattern is even more evident: 'Little vitality, mistaken upbringing, bachelorhood, produce the sceptic, but not necessarily: in order to save his scepticism many a sceptic marries, at least ideally, and becomes a believer.'[25]

9

A Naked Man among the Clothed

AT THE BEGINNING OF APRIL 1920, Kafka went to Merano in northern Italy for three months. Sitting on the balcony of the *Pension Ottoburg* he wrote the first letters to a 23-year-old Czech woman, whom he knew slightly from Prague and who had been living in Vienna for two years as the wife of a writer and banker. She had asked Kafka for permission to translate some of his writings into Czech. Her name was Milena Jesenská-Pollak.

Kafka was still engaged ('but without the prospect of marriage'[1] – a few months later the engagement was broken off) and 'to begin' with wanted only to 'lie down in a garden and extract from the disease ... as much sweetness as possible'.[2] In spite of their very rapidly growing correspondence, it seemed as if his wish could be fulfilled. Superficially at least, Milena Jesenská was more 'distant' from Kafka than any other woman in his life. She was 13 years younger, married and not Jewish (the only other non-Jewish woman in his life was the *Swiss woman*) but a Czech from an ancient, staunchly nationalistic family – her father, Jan Jesenská, was a jaw surgeon and professor at the Czech university in Prague.

Milena Jesenská had grown up without a mother from the age of 13. Her father, a self-centred tyrant for whom she had the same love-hatred as Kafka had for his, did not bother much about her.

Pension Ottoburg in Merano. In 1920, Kafka
wrote his letters to Milena from here.

She had attended the humanist Minerva *Gymnasium* for Young
Ladies founded by Czech intellectuals in 1891. The first generation
of Minerva graduates became part of the narrow stratum of eman-
cipated women in the subsequent Czechoslovak Republic. 'All'
Prague was then abuzz with that 'foray' into freedom, the pattern
for which was created principally by Milena Jesenská and two
friends, Staša Jilovská and Jarmila Reinerová: nocturnal excursions
to the cemetery, swimming across the Vltava with their clothes on,
reading of Knut Hamsun and Dostoevsky, first love among paint-
ers, writers and singers, flowing garments *à la* Isadora Duncan, the
study of medicine and music. She was extravagant and flamboyant,
which was probably a factor in her unconventional choice of partner
– Ernst Pollak, a Jew. (Of all her actions it was this that triggered
the fiercest disapproval from her father, who, for such 'follies', had

Milena Jesenská.

her committed to a nursing institution for nervous diseases. She was discharged only on reaching the age of majority, whereupon she married Ernst Pollak and moved with him to Vienna.)

Willy Haas described her as follows:

She sometimes struck one as like a noblewoman of the 16th or 17th century ... passionate, intrepid, cool and intelligent in her decisions, but reckless in the choice of means when her passion was involved – and during her youth it seems to have been involved almost all the time. As a friend she was inexhaustible, inexhaustible in kindness, inexhaustible in resources whose origin often remained enigmatic, but also inexhaustible in the claims she made on friends ... and as a lover ... During this period she squandered everything to an incredible degree: her life, money, feelings – her own feelings as well as those that were offered to her, and which she considered as her unconditional property to be disposed of as she pleased.[3]

And Margarete Buber-Neumann, a friend of her later years, wrote: 'As Kafka saw her, she, Milena, was the loving one. To her, love was the only truly great life ... She had no shyness and did not consider it shameful to experience feelings intensely. Love to her was something clear, something self-evident.'[4]

There is no doubt that Kafka at first shied away from Jesenská's demanding and rigorous love. In one of his first letters – and he returned to it time and again in subsequent letters – he told her of the 'discovery' of Dostoevsky, when Dmitri Grigorovich and Nikolay Nekrasov rang Dostoevsky's bell at three in the morning, after reading Dostoevsky's *Poor Folk*, hailing him as the greatest Russian writer, and how, when they had left, Dostoevsky stood by the window, crying: 'These wonderful people! How good and noble they are! And how base am I! ... If I were only to tell them they wouldn't believe it.'[5]

A few days later he wrote:

> ... and now I receive your letters, Milena. How shall I express
> the difference? A man lies in the filth and stench of his
> deathbed and there comes the angel of death, the most beatific
> of all angels, and looks at him. Can this man so much as dare
> to die? He turns over, hides himself even deeper in his bed,
> he's incapable of dying. In short: I don't believe what you say,
> Milena, and there's no way in which it could be proved to me
> – nor could anyone have proved it to Dostoevsky during that
> night, and my life lasts one night.[6]

Kafka was still trying to save Jesenská from himself – or, more accurately, to save himself from himself – yet his distress is obvious. Another 'warning letter':

> You must also consider, Milena, the kind of person who comes

to you, the 38-year journey lying behind me (and since I'm a Jew an even much longer one), and if at an apparently accidental turning of the road I see you, then, Milena, I cannot shout, nor does anything shout within me, nor do I say a thousand foolish things, they are not in me (I am omitting the other foolishness of which I have more than enough), and the fact that I'm kneeling I discover perhaps only through seeing your feet quite close before my eyes ...[7]

At about the same time, he wrote to Max Brod: 'She is a living fire, of a kind I have never seen before ... Yet at the same time she is extremely tender, courageous, bright, and commits everything she has to her sacrifice, or to put it another way perhaps, has gained everything she has by her sacrifice.'[8]

Jesenská asked Kafka to travel via Vienna on his return from Merano to Prague. Kafka hesitated, but in mid-June he wrote:

Whether you still wish to see me after my Wednesday, Thursday letters I cannot judge. My relationship to you I know (**you belong to me** even I were never to see you again) ... I know it insofar as it doesn't belong to the unfathomable realm of fear, but your relationship to me I don't know at all, it belongs entirely to fear. Neither do you know me, Milena, I repeat that.

For me, you see, what's happening is something prodigious. My world is tumbling down, my world is building itself up, watch out how you (I am this you) survive it. The tumbling down I don't deplore, it was in the process of tumbling, but what I do deplore is the building up of it. I deplore my lack of strength, deplore the being born, deplore the light of the sun.

How shall we continue to live? If you say 'Yes' to my letters, then you must not continue to live in Vienna, that's impossible.[9]

After this sentence, Kafka tells Jesenská a story relayed to him from Prague: a young man had poisoned himself on a night shift in his office; his wife arrived at the office in the morning with her friend (Willy Haas), but her husband was already in hospital and died before the two got there. He ended by writing: 'I repeat that you cannot remain in Vienna.' Jesenská knew what Kafka was demanding – she subsequently wrote to Max Brod: 'If I had gone to Prague with him that time, I would have remained what I was to him ... I was too weak to do the one and only thing that I knew would have helped him. That is my fault.'[10]

Both of them knew that her marriage was by then a sham. (It was actually dissolved a few years later.) Kafka visited her in Vienna for four days, of which Jesenská wrote: 'I knew his terror before I knew him ... In the four days that [he] was with me, he lost it. We laughed at it ... Not the slightest exertion was necessary: everything was simple and clear ... During those days his illness seemed to us something like a minor cold.'[11]

Kafka returned to Prague alone. A few weeks later they met once more, in *Gmünd*, the frontier station between Austria and Czechoslovakia; after that they did not see each other for a year. In the late autumn of 1920, Kafka wrote to Jesenská: 'I'd be terribly mistaken if the idea that we now cease writing to one another didn't turn out to be a good one. But I'm not mistaken, Milena.'[12] Neither of them quite stuck to this; in the winter of 1920/21 Kafka, writing from Matliary, repeated his request: 'Do not write and let us not see each other; I ask you only to quietly fulfil this request of mine; only on those conditions is survival possible for me; everything else continues the process of destruction.'[13]

Kafka could see no way out other than a clear decision from Jesenská; but he also realised that this was by no means as clear-cut as it was for him, and that he had no right to reiterate the alternative that he had confronted her with before his trip to Vienna. Yet to continue corresponding would have inevitably been a repetition of this demand.

They remained in touch: Jesenská visited Kafka in Prague several times in the autumn of 1921, and again in 1922. Kafka wrote short letters to her over the next few years, still from Berlin, with long pauses between them. In October 1921, Kafka handed over to her all his diaries – she already had the manuscript of *Amerika* and the 'Letter to his Father' – and never asked for them back. Given his general shyness, this was a remarkable (and unprecedented) proof of confidence. Jesenská, for her part, with an intuition like no other woman in Kafka's life, recognised it as such, even before he gave her his diaries:

> Obviously, we are capable of living because at some time or other we took refuge in lies, in blindness, in enthusiasm, in optimism, in some conviction or others, in pessimism or something of the sort. But he has never escaped to any such sheltering refuge, none at all. He is absolutely incapable of lying, just as he is incapable of getting drunk. He is without the slightest refuge or shelter. For that reason he is exposed to all those things against which we are protected. He is like a naked man among a multitude who are dressed ... And his asceticism is altogether unheroic ...
>
> All 'heroism' is a cowardly lie. One who conceives his asceticism as a means to an end is no true human being; the true human being is one who is compelled to asceticism by his terrible clarity of vision, purity and incapacity for compromise ... I know he does not resist **life**, but only **this kind of life**: that is what he resists.[14]

Kafka probably knew that it was 'too late' for such a love. In a letter to Milena in September 1920, shortly before ending their correspondence, he returned to the image of the deathbed, which he had mentioned in the spring, this time in the context of a quotation:

I'm reading a Chinese book ... it's concerned exclusively with death. A man lies on his deathbed and in the independence given him by the proximity of death, he says: 'I've spent my life trying to fight lust and to put an end to it.' Then a pupil mocks his teacher who speaks of nothing but death: 'You talk about death all the time but still you don't die.' 'I'll die all the same. I'm just singing my last song. One man's song is longer, another's shorter. The difference, however, can never be more than a few words.'

This is true, and it's unjust to smile about the hero who lies mortally wounded on the stage and sings an aria. We lie on the ground and sing for years.[15]

In the autumn of 1920, after a long break, Kafka began to write again: 'A few days ago I resumed that "war service" – or, more correctly, life "on manoeuvres", which I discovered years ago to be most suitable for myself at certain times.'[16] It was in 1912 that he had first embarked on his life 'on manoeuvres' – sleeping in the afternoon, writing at night. The family had moved into the Oppelt House, on the corner of *Altstädter Ring* (Staroměstské náměstí) and *Pariser Straße* (Pařížská, formerly Niklasstraße). There, between September and November 1920, in his third-floor room with a view of the turrets of St Nicholas's church, Kafka wrote a number of stories, such as 'The City Coat of Arms', 'Poseidon', 'Fellowship', 'At Night', 'The Problem of Our Laws', 'The Vulture' and 'The Top'.

In December, Kafka went to a tuberculosis sanatorium in Matliary in the Tatra Mountains – for the first time he seemed to want to be 'cured', though it is doubtful that, in his inner self, he really did. As far as we know, he wrote no prose in Matliary, but he did make the acquaintance of a young medical student – Robert Klopstock, 'very ambitious, clever, also highly literary ... He has a hunger for people, the way a born doctor does. Is anti-Zionist; his guides are Jesus and Dostoevsky.'[17] It was – at least initially – a paternal and didactic friendship: 'That poor medic. I have never yet witnessed such a demonic play from close to. One doesn't know, are these good or evil powers that are at work here, they certainly are monstrously strong. In the Middle Ages he would have been regarded as possessed. Yet he is a young person of 21, tall, broad, strong, ruddy-checked – extremely smart, truthful, unselfish, sensitive.'[18]

In this regard, Kafka's friendships during his final years (with the exception of his love for Milena Jesenská, but even this had such aspects) were all very much alike, in as much as they were all counselling, helping relationships with persons much younger than himself, often by ten or twenty years: with his sister Ottla, whom he advised on her agricultural plans and her marriage decisions; with Gustav Janouch (to whom we owe his *Conversations with Kafka*), who grew up in very unhappy family circumstances; with Minze Eisner, 'burdened with heavy mental health inheritance and an empty life',[19] whose acquaintance he had made in *Schelesen* (Želízy) in 1919 and with whom he corresponded, advising and consoling her, right up to his death; with his second fiancée Julie Wohryzek; and finally with Dora Diamant, the companion of his final six months, a young woman who had escaped to Germany from her orthodox Hasidic family in Poland. Kafka, himself carrying a heavy load, was genuinely something like an adviser and helper to the heavily laden during those years.

In September 1921, Kafka returned to Prague; his stay in Matliary had been in vain. In the course of the winter of 1921/22, he wrote the story 'First Sorrow' and a tone of finality enters his diary for the first time:

I have not shown the faintest firmness of resolve in the conduct of my life. It was as if I, like everyone else, had been given a point from which to trace the radius of a circle, and had then, like everyone else, to describe my perfect circle round this point. Instead I was forever starting my radius only constantly to be forced at once to break it off. (Examples: piano, violin, languages, Germanics, anti-Zionism, Zionism, Hebrew, gardening, carpentering, writing, marriage attempts, an apartment of my own.) The centre of my imaginary circle bristles with the beginnings of radii, there is no room left for a new attempt; no room means old age and weak nerves, and never to make another attempt means the end. If I sometimes prolonged the radius a little farther than usual, in the case of my law studies, say, or engagements, everything was made worse rather than better.[20]

A few weeks after writing these sentences in his diary, in February 1922, Kafka began to write down his attempt at some 'resolve in the conduct of [his] life' – the novel *The Castle*. The narrative concerns the efforts of a land surveyor, 'K', to 'describe a perfect circle' which is, in fact, merely a way of 'marking time', as Kafka writes of his own life a little earlier in the same diary entry. There is every reason to believe Brod's claim that the novel was to have concluded with the land surveyor dying of *fatigue*, hearing only on his deathbed that, *in view of certain circumstances*,[21] he would be permitted to settle in the village.

The 'autobiographical elements' in this novel are clearer than in any other: the parallels with Kafka's personal situation – that year he had finally parted with the Insurance Institute; his experiences in *Zürau*; the geography of the castle and the village (based on *Wossek*, his father's birthplace); the land surveyor as a kind of pariah, an image to which he kept returning in his letters and diaries; and finally his

The hotel in *Spindelmühle* in which Kafka
wrote the first parts of *The Castle*.

love affair with Milena Jesenská. Jesenská's husband Ernst ('he constantly had a string of other women beside Milena') is echoed in the
character of Klamm (a name that Kafka evidently derived from a pun
on the Christian name 'Ernst', which he had already mentioned in the
letters). It is through Frieda, who can never entirely detach herself
from Klamm, that the land surveyor tries to put down roots. One
final, very clear, allusion is the 'Herrenhof' inn where K. stays: this
was also the name of a Viennese café, a favourite haunt of Ernst Pollak,
Franz Werfel, Otto Pick, Egon Erwin Kisch and Otto Gross. Its literary habitués jokingly referred to it as 'Hurenhof' ('whorehouse').

Kafka began *The Castle* during a three-week stay in *Spindelmühle*,
continued to work on it in Prague (from March to June, during
which time he also wrote 'A Hunger Artist') and in *Planá* on the
Luschnitz (Lužnice) river (end of June to mid-September, where he

also wrote 'Investigations of a Dog').* In *Planá* he stayed with his sister Ottla: a diary entry from late September notes 'With some exceptions, a good period thanks to Ottla.' [22] But soon after his return, he wrote to Brod: '... I will evidently have to drop *The Castle* story forever.' [23]

During the winter of 1922/23 and the spring of 1923, Kafka was again living in Prague. There (apart from many things he later burnt) he wrote 'The Married Couple', 'Give it Up' and 'On Parables'. At the beginning of July, he travelled to *Müritz* on the Baltic with his sister Eli. There he visited a holiday colony of the Berlin Jewish People's Home – in 1916 he had supported Bauer's work in this home and sent her and the pupils some educational literature. He now made the acquaintance of one of the helpers, Dora Diamant, a young woman of about 25, whose Hasidic education and natural, naïve and helpful nature attracted him in equal measure. Several years earlier he had admitted that the stories of the Hasidim were the only part of Judaism that felt immediately familiar to him. He returned to Prague for a few days only, then spent a few weeks at *Schelesen* with his sister Ottla (with whom he apparently discussed his 'plan for life') and towards the end of September 1923 went to Berlin.

---

* *The Castle*. A man arrives in the dead of winter at a village over which there towers a castle. It belongs to one Count Westwest, but we see only the huge staff of bureaucrats who administer the village in his name. The new arrival, K, seeks employment as a land-surveyor, claiming he was summoned by the Castle, but there seems to he no record of his invitation: was he summoned through an administrative error or is he an impostor? K tries to settle in the village with the barmaid Frieda. But their emotional and erotic relationship is at risk, not only from the contempt in which the villagers hold any newcomer, but also from K's fixation on the Castle, which makes him desperate to confront an official responsible for his case. K's obsessive conflict with the Castle culminates in a chance encounter with a competent official, just when K is too exhausted to benefit from the meeting: 'Human strength,' says the official, 'extends only to a certain point, and perhaps that is just as well.'

Kafka standing in front of the Oppelt-House on the *Altstädter Ring*.
This picture was taken at about the time he wrote *The Castle*, 1922.

Dora Diamant.

Berlin had always been the only city Kafka might have been able to live in apart from Prague: in all his 'escape attempts' from his home city, Berlin invariably appeared as the first possible venue.* As early as 1914, he had written: 'Berlin is a much better city than Vienna, that dying giant village ... Even I feel the invigorating effect of Berlin, or rather I know that I would feel it if I moved there.'[24]

Kafka and Dora Diamant rented a flat in Steglitz and during the first few months Kafka was very happy. He had finally, against

---

*'When we were in Berlin, Kafka often went to the Steglitzer Park. Sometimes I would accompany him. One day we encountered a little girl, crying and evidently in great distress. Franz asked what had happened to her and we learned that she had lost her doll. Instantly he invented a plausible story: "Your doll has only gone on a journey, I know it, she has sent me a letter." The little girl was a little suspicious. "Have you got it with you?" "No, I've left it behind at home, but I'll bring it to you tomorrow." ... He got down to work in all earnestness, as though he was to create a literary work. He was in the same tense state as always when he sat at his desk...Franz had solved a child's small conflict through art – the most effective means at his personal disposal for bringing order into this world.' DORA DIAMANT

all opposition, enforced his departure from Prague, unexpectedly he had his own 'domesticity', and, albeit in a difficult period of high inflation, was living in a gratefully appreciated atmosphere of improvisation. To his sister Valli he wrote:

The table stands by the stove; I have just moved away from the fireside because it is too warm there, even for my perpetually cold back. My kerosene lamp burns marvellously, a masterpiece both of lamp-making and of purchasing. It has been assembled by borrowing and buying the separate pieces, though not by me, of course; how would I manage anything of the sort! It's a lamp with a burner as large as a teacup and a construction that makes it possible to light it without removing the chimney and shade. It has, in fact, only one flaw, that it won't burn without kerosene, but then we others are the same.[25]

To his friend Felix Weltsch, he described his new surroundings:

... my street is about the last half-urban one. Beyond it the countryside breaks up into gardens and villas, old, lush gardens. On warm evenings there is a strong fragrance, stronger than almost anything I have encountered elsewhere. Then in addition there are the great botanical gardens, a 15-minute walk from where I am, and the woods, where I have not yet been, are less than half an hour. So the setting for this little emigrant is beautiful.[26]

After six weeks he had to move – from *Miquelstraße* 8 to *Grunewaldstraße* 13: his landlady (Kafka portrayed her in 'A Little Woman') evidently had not liked his rather dubious 'household'.

In *Grunewaldstrasse*, he wrote a number of stories, but all, with the exception of 'The Burrow', were destroyed, some by Dora at

Kafka's request and under his eyes; others were subsequently lost. On one of his first visits, he told Max Brod that 'I have slipped away from my demons. This move to Berlin was magnificent, now they are looking for me and can't find me, at least for the moment.' [27] But in 'The Burrow' he writes: 'I have completed the construction of my burrow and I am pleased with the result ... I live in peace in the innermost chamber of my house, and meanwhile the enemy may be burrowing his way slowly and stealthily straight towards me.' [28] A few weeks after the move, Kafka, in his last letter to Milena Jesenská, wrote '... even here the old sufferings have found, attacked, and thrown me somewhat down'.[29]

His illness progressed rapidly over the next few months, exacerbated by his poor diet during that winter of inflation. In January 1924, he wrote to Max Brod:

> If the creature were not so decrepit, you could almost make a drawing of his appearance: On the left, Dora, say, supporting him; on the right, that man, say; some sort of 'scribbling' might stiffen his neck; now if only the ground beneath him were consolidated, the abyss in front of him filled in, the vultures around his head driven away, the storm in the skies above him quieted down if all that were to happen, then it might be just barely possible to go on for a while.[30]

At the beginning of March 1924, his condition worsened to such an extent that his Uncle Siegfried and Max Brod went to Berlin and brought Kafka back to Prague. His tuberculosis had attacked his larynx and there was now no hope of a cure. About that time when he said to Robert Klopstock, who had come to Prague, 'I think I began to investigate that animal squeaking at the right time'[31] – he wrote his last story, 'Josephine the Singer, or the Mouse Folk'. Its final sentences read: 'So perhaps we shall not miss so very much

The last photograph of
Franz Kafka, taken in Berlin
in 1923–4.

after all, while Josephine, redeemed from the earthly sorrows which
to her thinking lay in wait for all chosen spirits, will happily lose
herself in the numberless throng of the heroes of our people, and
soon, since we are no historians, will rise to the heights of redemp-
tion and be forgotten like all her brothers.'[32]

In early April, Kafka was taken to the Wiener Wald sanatorium,
from there to the Vienna University clinic, and towards the end of
April to the Sanatorium of a Doctor Hoffmann in Kierling near
Klosterneuburg, just north of Vienna. Robert Klopstock and Dora
Diamant were with him day and night, his lifelong friend Max Brod
visited him once more.

On 3 June 1924, one month before his 41st birthday, Franz Kafka

A Hunger Artist, a collection of stories published posthumously in 1924.

died. He was buried in Prague, the city he had always wanted to leave, but which held on to him, and whose world, in all its variety and strangeness (a strangeness which has distinct traits of modern alienation about it), he set down with terse precision. It was a world that came to represent modern alienation. With his only tool an obsessional commitment to unsparing truth, Kafka tried to record Prague's, and his own, situation. At the end of his life, with the same rigour, he judged his record to be full of gaps. In his will he requested that what remained of it be destroyed.*

---

*Kafka's manuscripts. Max Brod disregarded Kafka's stipulation in his will that his manuscripts should be destroyed. This act of disobedience preserved his work for us. Brod first edited *The Trial* (*Der Prozeß*), 1925, then *The Castle* (*Das Schloß*), 1926, and *Amerika*, which Kafka had called *Missing* or *The Man who Went Missing* (*Der Verschollene*), 1927. Shortly before the Nazis entered Prague, Brod escaped to Israel, saving the manuscripts a second time. The majority of these texts, the basis of the Critical Edition of Kafka's works, are now in the Bodleian Library in Oxford. A smaller number are in the German Literature Archive in Marbach.

Notes

Abbreviations used in Notes

Complete Novels: Franz Kafka, *The Complete Novels of Franz Kafka*, tr Willa and Edwin Muir (London: 1999).

Diaries: Franz Kafka, *The Diaries of Franz Kafka*, ed Max Brod, tr Joseph Kresh, Martin Greenberg, Hannah Arendt (London: 1948–9/1999).

L/Father: Franz Kafka, *Letter to his Father* (New York: 1970).

L/Felice: Franz Kafka, *Letters to Felice*, ed Erich Heller and Jürgen Born, tr James Stern and Elizabeth Duckworth (London: 1999).

L/Friends: Franz Kafka, *Letters to Friends, Family and Editors*, tr Richard and Clara Winston (New York: 1988).

L/Milena: Franz Kafka, *Letters to Milena*, ed Willy Haas, tr Tania and James Stern (London: 1953/1999).

Octavo Notebooks: Franz Kafka, *The Blue Octavo Notebooks* (Cambridge: 1991).

Stories: Franz Kafka, *The Complete Short Stories of Franz Kafka*, ed Nahum N Glatzer, various translators (London: 1933–54/1999).

Wagenbach, *Biographie*: Klaus Wagenbach, *Franz Kafka: Eine Biographie seiner Jugend, 1883–1912* (Berlin: 2006).

Introduction

1. *The Trial*, tr Willa and Edwin Muir (London: Gollancz, 1937), p 62; *The Trial*, tr Douglas Scott and Chris Waller (London: Picador, 1977), p 65.

2. Sales figures from Dieter Jakob, *Das Kafka-Bild in England: Darstellung – Dokumente – Bibliographie* (Oxford and Erlangen: 1971), pp 19–20. The introductory essay to Jakob's book was published separately in *Oxford German Studies*, 5 (1970), pp 90–143.

3. 'Introductory Note', Franz Kafka, *The Castle*, tr Willa and Edwin Muir (London: 1930), p viii.

4. Franz Kafka, *Nachgelassene Schriften und Fragmente II*, ed Jost Schillemeit (Frankfurt am Main: 1992), p 98.

5. Stephen Spender, *The Destructive Element* (London: 1935) quoted in Jakob, *Das Kafka-Bild*, p 219.

6. Emanuel Litvinoff, 'Kafka – the Logical Nightmare', *Spectator*, 10 September 1954, quoted in Jakob, *Das Kafka-Bild*, pp 476–8 (p 477).

7. *Spectator*, 23 July 1937, quoted in Jakob, *Das Kafka-Bild*, p 172.

8. 'A Letter from London', *The Masses* [New York], June 1938, 21–2, quoted in Jakob, *Das Kafka-Bild*, p 226.

9. Edmund Wilson, 'A Dissenting Opinion on Kafka', *New Yorker*, 26 July 1947, 58–64; reprinted in his *Classics and Commercials* (London: 1951); quoted in Jakob, *Das Kafka-Bild*, p 464.

10. See Shimon Sandbank, *After Kafka: The Influence of Kafka's Fiction* (Athens and London: 1989).

11. Jorge Luis Borges, *Labyrinths* (Harmondsworth: 1970), p 58.

12. Walter Benjamin, 'Franz Kafka: On the Tenth Anniversary of his Death', in *Illuminations*, tr. Harry Zohn (London: 1970).

13. Julian Symons, *The Thirties* (London: 1960), quoted in Jakob, *Das Kafka-Bild*, p 207.

14. Alasdair Gray, *Lanark* (Edinburgh: 1981), p 491.

15. Nadine Gordimer, 'Letter from his Father', in *Something Out There* (London: 1984).

16. 'The Matliary Diary', in J P Stern (ed), *The World of Franz Kafka* (London: 1980), pp 238–50. Anyone familiar with Frederic Manning's great First World War novel, variously entitled *Her Privates We* and *The Middle Parts of Fortune*, will recognise how far Stern's Kafka is modelled on Manning's central character Bourne.

17. Alan Bennett, 'Kafka at Las Vegas', in his *Writing Home*, rev edn (London: 1997), p 517.

18. Roy Fuller, 'A Normal Enough Dog: Kafka and the Office', in Stern (ed), *The World of Franz Kafka*, pp 191–201 (p 207).

19. See Martin Brady and Helen Hughes, 'Kafka adapted to film', in Julian Preece (ed), *The Cambridge Companion to Kafka* (Cambridge: 2002), pp 226–41.

20. See Raymond Armstrong, *Kafka and Pinter: Shadow Boxing* (Basingstoke: 1999), Chapter 2.

21. Alan Bennett, *Two Kafka Plays* (London: 1987), p 15.

1: Fame – Too Late for the Author

1. Franz Kafka, *The Complete Short Stories*, ed Nahum N Glatzer, various translators (London: 1983/1999), p 89.

2. Franz Kafka, *The Transformation and Other Stories*, tr Malcolm Pasley (London: 1992), p 161.

3. *Diaries*, p 235.

2: The Son of a Shopkeeper, Lost in Prague

1. *L/Father*, p 125.

2. *L/Milena*, p 63.

3. *Diaries*, pp 152f.

4. From the notebooks of Hélène Zylberberg in the German Literature Archive in Marbach.

5. *L/Friends*, p 410.

6. *L/Friends*, p 309.

7. *L/Father*, p 65.

8. *L/Father*, p 11.

9. *L/Father*, p 13.

10. Gustav Janouch, *Conversations with Kafka*, tr Goronwy Rees (London, Melbourne, New York: 1985), p 80, translation modified.

11. Friedrich Thieberger in *Als Kafka Mir Entgegenkam: Erinnerungen an Franz Kafka*, ed Hans-Gerd Koch (Berlin: 1995), p 126.

12. *L/Milena*, pp 52f.

13. *L/Father*, pp 27, 55.

14. *L/Felice*, p 398.

15. *L/Friends*, p 297.

16. *L/Father*, p 63.

17. *L/Father*, p 15.

18. *Diaries*, p 123.

19. *L/Father*, p 21.

20. *Diaries*, p 160.

21. *L/Friends*, pp 292f.

3: What does a Boy Learn at an Imperial and Royal Secondary School?

1. Fritz Mauthner, *Erinnerungen I* (Munich: 1918), pp 94f.

2. 'Die Götter Griechenlands', in Friedrich Schiller, *Sämtliche Werke*, ed Gerhard Fricke and Herbert G Göpfe (Munich: 1958) vol I, pp 164, 166.

3. *L/Father*, pp 77f.

4. *L/Father*, p 81.
5. *L/Father*, p 79.
6. Mauthner, *Erinnerungen I*, p 118.
7. Janouch, *Conversations*, p 115.
8. *Diaries*, pp 158f.
9. See Wagenbach, *Biographie*, pp 268f.
10. *Diaries*, p 367.
11. Franz Kafka, *Wedding Preparations in the Country and Other Posthumous Writings* (London: 1954), pp 221f.
12. *L/Father*, p 89.
13. *L/Friends*, p 270.
14. *L/Friends*, p 362.
15. *Diaries*, p 222.
16. *Diaries*, p 20.
17. *Diaries*, p 146.
18. *L/Father*, p 93: translation modified.
19. *Diaries*, p 405.
20. To Oskar Pollak. See Max Brod, *Franz Kafka* (Cambridge, MA: 1995), p 44.
21. *Diaries*, p 37.
22. *Diaries*, p 405.
23. *Octavo Notebooks*, p 56.
24. *L/Friends*, p 12.
25. *L/Friends*, p 9.
26. *Stories*, p 384.
27. Johann Wolfgang von Goethe, *Torquato Tasso*, tr Alan Brownjohn (London: 1985), p 37.

4: University, Society and Language in the Capital of Bohemia

1. *L/Father*, p 95.

2. *L/Friends*, pp 25f.
3. Brod, *Kafka*, p 44.
4. *L/Friends*, pp 15f.
5. *L/Friends*, p 17, translation modified.
6. *Stories*, p 20.
7. *L/Friends*, p 17.
8. Brod, *Kafka*, p 44, translation modified.
9. Hugo von Hofmannsthal, *Prosa II* (Frankfurt: 1951), p 95.
10. *Stories*, p 25.
11. *Stories*, p 21.
12. *Stories*, p 24.
13. *Stories*, p 22.
14. Franz Kafka, *The Great Wall of China* (New York: 1970), pp 153f.
15. *L/Friends*, p 17.
16. *L/Friends*, p 17.
17. *Stories*, p 72.
18. *Octavo Notebooks*, p 14.
19. *L/Friends*, pp 19f.
20. *L/Friends*, p 117.
21. *Stories*, pp 73f.
22. *L/Friends*, p 21.
23. *L/Friends*, p 25.
24. *L/Friends*, p 35.
25. *L/Friends*, p 5.
26. See Brod, *Kafka*, p 88, letter No 5 of May 1907.
27. *Diaries*, p 263.
28. See Peter Demetz, *René Rilkes Prager Jahre* (Düsseldorf: 1953), p 142.
29. See Rilke's story 'König Bohusch'.
30. Theodor Herzl, *Die entschwundenen Zeiten* (Vienna: 1897).
31. *L/Father*, p 91.

32. *Octavo Notebooks*, p 59.
33. *Diaries*, p 396.
34. Paul Leppin, in *Das jüdische Prag* (Prague: 1917), pp 5f.
35. Franz Werfel, *Embezzled Heaven* (London: 1940).
36. Paul Leppin, *Daniel Jesus* (Leipzig: 1905), p 111.
37. Rainer Maria Rilke, *The Notebooks of Malte Laurids Brigge*, tr
    John Linton (London: 1950), pp 38, 46.
38. Gustav Meyrink, *Der violette Tod*.
39. Brod, *Kafka*, p 44.
40. Mauthner, *Erinnerungen I*, p 51.
41. Franz Werfel, *Der Weltfreund* (Berlin: 1912), p 97.
42. *Stories*, p 225.
43. Max Brod, *Schloss Nornepygge* (Stuttgart: 1908), p 473.
44. *L/Milena*, p 26.
45. *Diaries*, p 371.

5: 'Description of a Struggle': the Insurance Official, his Job, his Plans and his Journeys

1. *L/Friends*, pp 35f.
2. *L/Friends*, p 29.
3. *Diaries*, p 326.
4. Brod, *Kafka*, pp 66f.
5. *Diaries*, pp 90, 162.
6. *L/Friends*, p 25.
7. Stefan Zweig, *Max Brod: 'Witiko' II* (1929), pp 124f.
8. *Stories*, pp 53, 55f.
9. *Diaries*, p 231.
10. Brod, *Kafka*, pp 101f; see also Hans-Gerd Koch (ed), *Als Kafka
    mir entgegenkam: Erinnerungen an Franz Kafka* (Berlin: 1995),
    p 89.
11. Ottokar Wirth, in a letter to the author.

12. Wagenbach, *Biographie*, p 149.

13. Wagenbach, *Biographie*, p 329.

14. Wagenbach, *Biographie*, p 305.

15. Wagenbach, *Biographie*, p 299.

16. *Bericht der Arbeiter-Unfall-Versicherungs-Anstalt für das Königreich Böhmen über ihre Tätigkeit während der Zeit vom 1. Jänner bis 31 Dezember 1909* (Prague: 1910), pp 7f. See Wagenbach, *Biographie*, p 225. Quoted from Brod, *Kafka*, pp 83f.

17. Gustav Janouch, *Conversations with Kafka*, tr Goronwy Rees (London, Melbourne, New York: 1985), p 105.

18. Brod, *Kafka*, p 82.

19. František Soukup, speech in parliament, *Bohemia*, 27 January 1909.

20. Max Brod, *Zauberreich der Liebe* (Berlin: 1928), p 95.

21. Brod, *Kafka*, p 84.

22. *Diaries*, p 95.

23. Wagenbach, *Biographie*, pp 180f.

24. *L/Friends*, p 147.

25. *L/Friends*, p 349.

26. *L/Friends*, pp 82f.

27. *L/Friends*, p 387.

28. *Diaries*, p 333.

6: The Only Way to Write!

1. Franz Kafka, *Ein Landarzt und andere Drucke zu Lebzeiten* (Frankfurt: 1994), p 325.

2. *Diaries*, pp 212f, translation modified.

3. *L/Milena*, p 152.

4. *L/Friends, Diaries*.

5. Søren Kierkegaard, *Der Begriff der Angst*, 3rd chapter, § 3.

6. *Diaries*, p 230.
7. *L/Friends*, p 334.
8. *L/Friends*, pp 333f.
9. *L/Friends*, p 340.
10. Karl Kraus, *Sprüche und Widersprüche* (Munich: 1914), p 41.
11. Franz Werfel, *Twilight of a World*, tr H T Lowe-Porter (New York: 1957), pp 448f.
12. *L/Friends*, p 45.
13. *Complete Novels*, p 67.
14. Franz Kafka, *The Trial*, tr Willa and Edwin Muir (London: 1935/1953), p 121.
15. *Complete Novels*, p 299.
16. *L/Friends*, p 28.
17. *L/Father*, p 121.
18. *Diaries*, p 207.
19. *L/Friends*, p 90.
20. Brod, *Kafka*, p 148. Only in 1963 edition.
21. *L/Milena*, p 148.
22. See *Diaries*, p 104. 'Grosser Lärm' in *Herder-Blätter* I, 4/5, October 1912.
23. *L/Friends*, p 193.
24. Hans Heilmann, *Chinesische Lyrik vom 12. Jahrhundert v. Chr. bis zur Gegenwart* (Munich: 1905).
25. *Diaries*, p 385.

7: Life or Literature? Kafka's Engagements and *The Trial*

1. *Diaries*, p 260.
2. *Diaries*, p 222.
3. *Diaries*, pp 225f.
4. *Diaries*, p 229.
5. *Diaries*, pp 230f.

6. *L/Felice*, p 355.
7. *Diaries*, p 329.
8. *Diaries*, p 232.
9. *L/Friends*, p 117.
10. *Diaries*, p 412.
11. *Diaries*, p 234.
12. *Diaries*, p 231.
13. *Diaries*, p 262.
14. *Diaries*, p 263.
15. *Diaries*, p 275.
16. *L/Felice*, p 451.
17. *Diaries*, p 302.
18. *Diaries*, p 302.
19. *Diaries*, p 302.
20. *Diaries*, p 303.
21. *Diaries*, p 293.
22. *Diaries*, p 314.
23. *Diaries*, p 314.
24. *Diaries*, p 321. Franz Kafka, *The Trial*, tr Willa and Edwin Muir (London: 1935/1953), p 235.
25. *Diaries*, pp 315f.
26. *L/Felice*, p 474.
27. *Diaries*, p 328.
28. *Diaries*, p 361.
29. *Diaries*, p 329.
30. *Diaries*, p 364.
31. In manuscript only, at *Diaries*, p 365.
32. *L/Friends*, pp 117f.
33. *L/Felice*, p 561.
34. *Diaries*, pp 331, 333.
35. *L/Felice*, p 562.
36. *Stories*, p 240.

37. Brod, *Kafka*, p 157.
38. *L/Friends*, pp 133, 134.
39. *Octavo Notebooks*, p 62.
40. *Diaries*, pp 383f.

8. The Wound

1. *L/Friends*, p 137.
2. *Stories*, p 225.
3. *L/Milena*, p 20.
4. *L/Friends*, p 136, translation modified.
5. Brod, *Kafka*, p 164.
6. *L/Friends*, pp 137f, 142.
7. *Diaries*, p 385.
8. Brod, *Kafka*, pp 166f.
9. Franz Kafka, *Letters to Ottla and the Family*, tr Richard and Clara Winston (New York: 1982), p 24.
10. *Diaries*, p 325.
11. *Diaries*, p 339.
12. *Diaries*, p 372.
13. *Diaries*, p 372, translation modified.
14. Kafka, *Letters to Ottla and the Family*, pp 25f.
15. *Diaries*, pp 386f.
16. *Diaries*, p 388.
17. *Diaries*, p 388.
18. Max Brod's diary, 1 July 1918. Unpublished, kept in Tel Aviv.
19. *L/Milena*, p 32.
20. Letter to Julie Wohryzek's sister, 24 November 1919. See Jürgen Born and others, *Kafka-Symposion* (Berlin: 1965), pp 45f and Anthony Northey, 'Julie Wohryzek' in *Freibeuter* 59 (1994).
21. *L/Milena*, p 32.
22. *L/Father*, p 87.

23. *L/Father*, p 109.

24. *L/Father*, p 107.

25. *L/Father*, p 275.

9: A Naked Man among the Clothed

1. *L/Milena*, p 21.

2. *L/Milena*, pp 21, 22.

3. *L/Milena*, pp 8f, in Haas's preface.

4. Margarete Buber-Neumann, *Kafkas Freundin Milena* (Munich: 1963), p 98.

5. *L/Milena*, p 23, translation modified.

6. *L/Milena*, p 31.

7. *L/Milena*, p 38.

8. *L/Friends*, p 237.

9. *L/Milena*, p 57, translation modified.

10. Brod, *Kafka*, pp 233f.

11. Brod, *Kafka*, p 233.

12. *L/Milena*, p 177.

13. See Brod, *Kafka*, pp 231f.

14. Brod, *Kafka*, pp 230, 234.

15. *L/Milena*, pp 168f.

16. *L/Milena*, p 148.

17. *L/Friends*, p 259.

18. Kafka, *Letters to Ottla and the Family*, pp 66f.

19. Hans-Gerd Koch (ed), *Als Kafka mir entgegenkam: Erinnerungen an Franz Kafka* (Berlin: 1995), p 145.

20. *Diaries*, p 404.

21. See Max Brod's 'Afterword' to his edition of *The Castle*.

22. *Diaries*, p 422.

23. *L/Friends*, p 357.

24. *L/Felice*, p 436.

25. *L/Friends*, p 395.
26. *L/Friends*, p 386.
27. Brod, *Kafka*, p 197.
28. *Stories*, pp 325f.
29. *L/Milena*, p 189.
30. *L/Friends*, p 405.
31. *L/Friends*, p 495.
32. *Stories*, p 376.

Further Reading

Adler, Jeremy, *Franz Kafka* (London: 2001).

Alter, Robert, *Necessary Angels: Tradition and Modernity in Kafka, Benjamin and Scholem* (Cambridge, MA: 1991).

Anderson, Mark (ed), *Reading Kafka: Prague, Politics and the Fin de Siècle* (New York: 1989).

——, *Kafka's Clothes: Ornament and Aestheticism in the Habsburg Fin de Siècle* (Oxford: 1992).

Boa, Elizabeth, *Kafka: Gender, Class and Race in the Letters and Fictions* (Oxford: 1996).

Dodd, W J, *Kafka and Dostoevsky: The Shaping of Influence* (London: 1992).

——(ed), *The Metamorphosis, The Trial and The Castle*, Modern Literatures in Perspective (London and New York: 1995).

Dowden, Stephen D, *Kafka's Castle and the Critical Imagination* (Columbia, SC: 1995).

Gilman, Sander L, *Franz Kafka, the Jewish Patient* (London and New York: 1995).

Glatzer, Nahum N, *The Loves of Franz Kafka* (New York: 1986).

Grandin, John M, *Kafka's Prussian Advocate: A Study of the Influence of Heinrich von Kleist on Franz Kafka* (Columbia, SC: 1987).

Hayman, Ronald, *'K'. A Biography of Kafka* (London: 1981).

Kafka's Prague

Heidsieck, Arnold, *The Intellectual Contexts of Kafka's Fiction: Philosophy, Law, Religion* (Columbia, SC: 1994).

Hockaday, Mary, *Kafka, Love and Courage: The Life of Milena Jesenská* (London: 1995).

Koelb, Clayton, *Kafka's Rhetoric: The Passion of Reading* (Ithaca and London: 1989).

Marson, Erich L, *Kafka's Trial: The Case against Josef K.* (St Lucia, Queensland: 1975).

Northey, Anthony, *Kafka's Relatives: Their Lives and His Writing* (New Haven and London: 1991).

Pawel, Ernst, *The Nightmare of Reason: A Life of Franz Kafka* (New York: 1984).

Preece, Julian (ed), *The Cambridge Companion to Kafka* (Cambridge: 2002).

Robertson, Ritchie, *Kafka: Judaism, Politics, and Literature* (Oxford: 1985).

Sheppard, Richard, *On Kafka's Castle: A Study* (London: 1973).

Spector, Scott, *Prague Territories: National Conflict and Cultural Innovation in Franz Kafka's fin de Siècle* (Berkeley, Los Angeles, and London: 2000).

Speirs, Ronald, and Beatrice Sandberg, *Franz Kafka*, Macmillan Modern Novelists (London: 1997).

Unseld, Joachim, *Franz Kafka: A Writer's Life*, tr Paul F Dvorak (Riverside, CA: 1997).

186

Index